DINOSAUR LAKE

The Story of the Purgatoire Valley Dinosaur Tracksite Area

Martin G. Lockley, Barbara J. Fillmore, Lori Marquardt

Artwork by Paul Koroshetz unless otherwise noted
Historical photos and artwork courtesy of the Colorado
    Historical Society
Photos provided by the authors unless otherwise noted
Layout and design by Lori Marquardt,
    University of Colorado at Denver
    Dinosaur Trackers Research Group

FIGURE CREDITS

These figures are © copyrighted, all rights reserved: page vi—Louie Psihoyos; pages 2 (bottom), 4, 8 (top), 9, 22-23, 25 (top), 26, 27 (bottom), 28 (top and bottom right), 29 (top and bottom left), 31-35, 36 (bottom), 37, 39, 41, 45-47 (top and bottom left), 48 (bottom), 52 (top), 53 (bottom)-55 (top and center)—Dr. Martin Lockley, University of Colorado at Denver; page 42—Cambridge University Press, *Tracking Dinosaurs* by Martin Lockley, figure number 14.5; pages 3, 5, 12, 15, 17 (top), 25 (bottom), 47 (bottom right), 51, and cover art—Paul Koroshetz; pages 11, 28 (bottom left), 29 (bottom right), 36 (top), 44, 52 (center and bottom)—University of Colorado Dinosaur Tracking exhibit; pages 13, 19, 27 (top)—Barbara J. Fillmore; pages 14 (F32609), 16 (F33937), 17 (bottom) (F160), 18 (F2, 352WPA, F1535)—courtesy, Colorado Historical Society; page 21—Pueblo Star-Journal; page 24—John Stewart MacClary's Journal of the expedition to the Purgatoire site on April 25, 1937; page 38—adapted from Charles Sternberg, Canadian Geological Survey, 1932; page 43—Douglas Henderson; page 48—adapted from *The Illustrated Encyclopedia of Dinosaurs* by Dr. David Norman; page 53 (top)—John Sibbick.

These figures produced by state and federal agencies are in the public domain: pages 55 (bottom)-57—U.S. Forest Service; pages 2 (top), 7, 58, 59 (bottom)—adapted from the U.S. Forest Service Comanche National Grassland Visitor Map; page 8 (bottom)—adapted from U.S. Geological Survey, La Junta Quadrangle map I-560; page 20—Jack Rathbone for the Colorado Geological Survey.

Colorado Geological Survey,
1313 Sherman Street, Room 715
Denver, Colorado 80203
1997

ISBN 1-884216-53-6

CONTENTS

ACKNOWLEDGEMENTS

This project was funded in part by the U.S. Geological Survey, through a Department of the Interior's Excellence in Education Initiative grant. Substantial material and in kind contributions to the research and production phases were made by the University of Colorado at Denver Dinosaur Trackers Research Group and the U.S.D.A. Forest Service. Coordination of the project was facilitated by a Memorandum of Understanding among the U.S. Forest Service, Department of Agriculture, and the U.S. Geological Survey, Department of the Interior, Bureau of Land Management, Department of the Interior, and National Park Service, Department of the Interior, for management of fossils on public lands. This publication represents an example of the scientific documentation of a valuable fossil resource as a cooperative endeavor among the subject agencies in coordination with academia. Much of the initial research was conducted by the University of Colorado at Denver Dinosaur Trackers Research Group with sponsorship from the University of Colorado and the National Science Foundation.

The authors wish to thank the following people and organizations for their assistance: Tom Warren, Environmental Director at Fort Carson, for unwavering commitment to the protection and conservation of the Picket Wire's fragile resources; Chuck L. Pillmore, U.S. Geological Survey, Scientist Emeritus, for initiating the project; Debra Dandridge and David M. Pieper, U.S. Forest Service, for guidance, information, field trips to the dinosaur tracksite area and review of the guide; Dave Wolf and the U.S. Forest Service Geometronics Group for their support with maps and technology; Thomas W. Henry, U.S. Geological Survey, for information and review of the guide; Rusty Dersch and Jeff Bruggink, U.S. Forest Service, for information; Vicki Cowart, Director and State Geologist and the staff of the Colorado Geological Survey for editing, publishing, and marketing the manuscript; and Vera Sable, for typing.

Former members of the C.U. Denver Dinosaur Trackers Research Group, especially Nancy Prince and Karen Houck, have also made substantial contributions to research in this area. The Research Group continues to conduct field studies in the area with the sponsorship of the U.S. Forest Service. We thank Cathleen May and Al Kane for their support in this regard.

We also thank Louie Psihoyos for permission to use his spectacular early-morning shot for educational and promotional purposes.

This book is dedicated to Betty Jo Hart and John Stewart MacClary, who brought knowledge of dinosaur tracks "out of Purgatory."

..and departing, leave behind us
footprints on the sands of time."

Longfellow: A Psalm of Life]

An Introduction

The Purgatoire River rises in the Rocky Mountains west of Trinidad, Colorado, and flows northeast across the southern High Plains for a distance of about 150 miles to its confluence with the Arkansas River just east of Las Animas. Although a sparsely populated and little known area, the Purgatoire Valley is one of the most beautiful locations on the High Plains. A serious study of the cultural history, geology, and natural history of this river valley could easily run to several volumes and is beyond the scope of this guidebook. Instead, we focus on the story of one small stretch of this valley known as Picket Wire Canyonlands. The Picket Wire Canyonlands lie within the Comanche National Grasslands, approximately 23 miles south of the town of La Junta in southeastern Colorado. The area, currently managed by the U.S.D.A. Forest Service, is rich in history, flora and fauna, and above all has a unique paleontological heritage. It contains the largest dinosaur tracksite currently known in North America. The tracksite is located in the northern portion of the Canyonlands, and the track-bearing rock is situated both within—and on—the banks of the Purgatoire River.

In recent years there has been a resurgence of interest in dinosaur tracks, and general interest in dinosaurs has reached fever pitch. As a result, the Purgatoire Tracksite has been featured in nationally and internationally distributed magazine articles and television documentaries about dinosaurs, as well as in scientific papers and books. It is therefore a good time to review what is known about this important site, summarize its history, the current state of knowledge, and probable future.

Location of the Comanche National Grasslands.

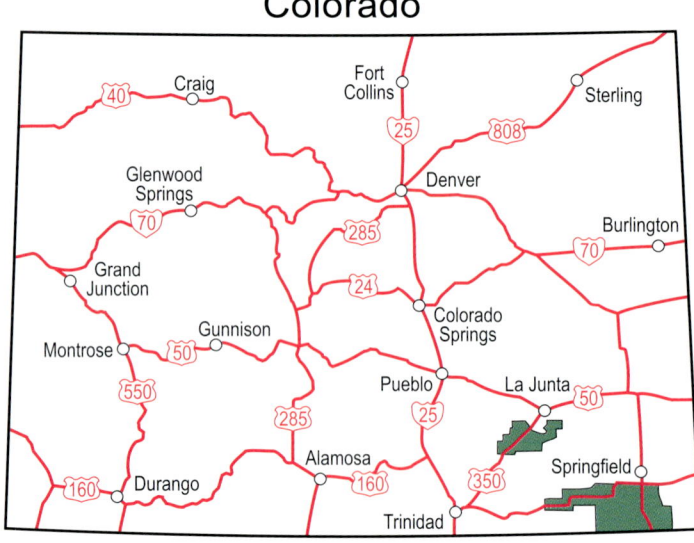

Colorado

Oblique view of the tracksite.

The Purgatoire Tracksite is associated with strata (layers of rock) known as the Morrison Formation. This geologic strata, dating from the Late Jurassic Epoch—about 150-million years ago—is one of the most famous dinosaur-bearing deposits in the world, containing well-known fossil sites such as Dinosaur National Monument. First discovered in 1877, near Morrison, Colorado, the formation quickly yielded some of the world's best known dinosaurs (such as *Stegosaurus* and *Apatosaurus*—better known as "Brontosaurus") in the form of partial or complete skeletons used to stock the world's museums and introduce dinosaurs to a broad international audience.

The late 1800s were a period of intensive digging for dinosaurs. The activity of this time was dubbed the "Bone Wars" due to an intense rivalry that developed between Edward Cope and Othniel C. Marsh, two of North America's most famous 19th century paleontologists. As a result of this "dinosaur bone rush," little attention was paid to tracks until the 20th century. It was not until the 1930s that the Purgatoire site, and several other important dinosaur tracksites in the western United States were discovered. Even then, the full potential and significance of the tracksites were not realized.

The perception of tracks as relatively insignificant fossil evidence began to change in the 1980s, in the wake of the so-called "dinosaur renaissance." During this time dinosaurs acquired a new image as agile and intelligent creatures rather than plodding behemoths. Because tracks are made by live creatures, they are obviously a very dynamic type of evidence that sheds light on animal locomotion, speed, behavior, and ecology. The result of this reawakening of scientific interest was that previously known fossil footprint sites were reinvestigated and many new sites discovered.

The Purgatoire Tracksite was studied in detail for the first time in 1982 and was described in scientific literature. The Morrison Formation had previously been considered bone-rich and track-poor, but it soon became clear that a very significant track record existed. The Purgatoire site alone was shown to yield six track-bearing layers containing at least 1,300 footprints, representing a minimum of 100 animals, mainly sauropods and theropods. Sauropods are the group of large, long-necked creatures that are commonly referred to in general as "brontosaurs." Theropods are the two-legged, carnivorous dinosaurs such as *Allosaurus*. These tracks represent a larger number of dinosaurs than

has been found at almost any other single dinosaur site in the Morrison Formation.

The site is currently the largest continuously mapped fossil footprint site in North America—perhaps the world. Among the more significant discoveries from the Purgatoire Tracksite are: some of the world's longest trackways; the world's first reported brontosaur tracks; evidence of herding or social behavior; and evidence that brontosaurs trampled and extensively disturbed the soils beneath their feet. The fossil evidence and rock record also show that the tracksite area represents a lake shoreline environment preserving evidence of a very distinctive 150-million-year-old lake ecosystem. For this reason, this ancient environment has been dubbed "Dinosaur Lake."

These then are some of the interesting facts that make the Purgatoire Tracksite a unique part of the national natural heritage. The following sections outline: the natural setting, geology, and history of the area; a detailed account of the fossil footprints and their significance; the status of erosion problems; and the value of the site for public education. A Visitor's Guide to the Purgatoire Tracksite area will also be available.

Special legislation mandates the preservation and conservation of the fragile and unique resources at the Puratoire Tracksite and in the Picket Wire Canyonlands. Fossils, trackways, artifacts, and other resources should not be removed or damaged. It requires thoughtful planning to ensure a safe and educational visit in the semi-arid environment of the Comanche National Grasslands. Please keep the area beautiful and complete for our enjoyment today, and for future generations who will visit the area tomorrow.

The Purgatoire Valley

The Area

Today and Yesterday

THE NATURAL SETTING

The dinosaur tracksite lies along the Purgatoire River within the flood-plain of a wide canyon, an area with beautiful scenery and an appealing landscape. The terrain varies from steep cliff walls to broad floodplains with the river as the central focus. Vegetation on the higher floodplain consists of short grasses and different cactus species such as cholla and prickly pear, while willows, tamarisk, sedges, and cotton-wood trees lie along the lower floodplain. Other plants to be found in the area are wolfberry, chinese lantern, salt bush, yucca, and devil's claw. Juniper generally grows on steep canyon walls, and pinyon and juniper domi-nate the woodland and rimrock areas.

Non-native kochia and tamarisk—or "salt cedar"—are both considered weeds and often dominate the native willows, grasses, and cottonwoods. Ironically, plants such as the tamarisk were brought into the area in the 1930s to control erosion. Now, these non-native plants contribute to the potential for severe fire hazards in the canyon and adversely impact the area's riparian zones and native vegetation.

In April of 1996, a fire burned approximately 9300 acres, 6,200 acres in the Comanche National Grasslands itself. This fire burned much of the bottom-land (floodplain) in the canyon. The U.S. Forest Service feels that even though some short-term damage was done, this natural agent of renewal was mostly beneficial instead of destructive. They are using this as an opportunity to reseed the area with native plants. Many of the undesirable weeds can bounce back from their root system, but hopefully the efforts made to replace the weeds will be successful in the long-term.

Wild animal groups include mule and white tail deer, big horn sheep, pronghorn antelope, coyote, fox, bobcat, badger, cottontail and jackrabbits, and rodents of various kinds. Birds such as quail, mountain bluebirds, roadrunners, warblers, Bewick's wren, various woodpeckers, wild turkey, bald and golden eagles, owls, and hawks use the various canyon habitats.

Many species of amphibians and reptiles, including bullsnakes, rattlesnakes, turtles, and a variety of lizards and frogs, are also found. Eleven species of native fishes, such as black bullhead, flathead chub, and green sunfish occupy the Purgatoire River, although the river is classified as a Limited Fishery Resource due to lack of habitat in the limestone river bottom and relatively sparse shoreline vegetation. The Purgatoire River has a high mineral and saline content due to gypsum-bearing bedrock and limestone and shale soils, so only fish that evolved in this type of environment live there. The river is therefore valuable as an example of a mature riparian habitat. Riparian areas are ecological units with distinctive vegetation, landform, soil, and water regimes associated with rivers or lakes.

No summary of the flora and fauna would be complete without some mention of the insects and arthropods that actually outnumber all other creatures. The venomous scorpions and tarantulas intrigue us and sometimes engender feelings of fear and repulsion. In reality, very few people are ever bitten by these creatures, and one is unlikely to encounter scorpions unless one goes looking for them in crevices and under rocks. The larger tarantulas are more obvious and can often be spotted crossing roads or open ground, especially in the fall. At this time they fall prey to the deadly tarantula hawk wasp—a menacing shiny black insect with blood red wings—that paralyzes its victim and drags it off into a burrow. There it lays its eggs on the still-live body—a macabre strategy to provide a food supply for its young when they hatch. In comparison with the wasp, the fuzzy tarantula appears an unhappy victim. For those interested in entomology, there are opportunities to observe dragonflies, dung beetles, and a myriad of other insects and arthropods that inhabit the canyonlands.

The climate in the basin is semi-arid, with an average precipitation of approximately 30 centimeters (12 inches) per year. During the summer months, temperatures frequently exceed 43 degrees Celsius (110 degrees Fahrenheit), and large thunderstorms can cause occasionally severe flooding. Flash floods on the Purgatoire River and in arroyos of the side canyons can cause erosion and have been known to damage surfaces that contain dinosaur tracks.

The natural setting has not always been as it is today. As little as 150 years ago, the Purgatoire River was a lush river oasis—created by the damming of the river by an abundant beaver population. This damming caused pooling of the waters and created marshy areas rich in animal and plant life. The intense hunting of the beaver by trappers eliminated the dams, and farming and grazing practices polluted the waters and stripped the soil, adding to the erosional features seen today. Beaver have not been completely eliminated from the Purgatoire Valley however, and it is easy to find their tracks and evidence of their activity in the form of felled trees and numerous logs bearing distinctive gnawing traces.

THE GEOLOGIC SETTING

The Picket Wire Canyonlands is divided into four geographically separate areas referred to as the Southern, Middle, and Northern Tracts, and the Upper Tier. The dinosaur tracksite is located in the Northern Tract and this area is referred to as the Purgatoire Tracksite throughout this book.

Rocks of Late Paleozoic (Permian) and Mesozoic (Triassic, Jurassic, and Cretaceous) age are exposed in the four areas. The geology varies considerably among the areas, as shown in the figure on page 8, which compares the Middle Tract with the Northern Tract. Late Paleozoic rocks are exposed only in the Middle Tract where uplift has occurred in the Black Hills region nearby. The Northern and Southern Tracts reveal only Jurassic and Cretaceous rocks. The Upper Tier rocks are poorly exposed and are exclusively Cretaceous in age. In the 1960s, Glen Scott of the U.S. Geological Survey produced the first geological map of the area.

In the Northern Tract, where the dinosaur tracksite is located, the bottom of the valley floor and the

Map of the four areas within the Picket Wire Canyonlands.

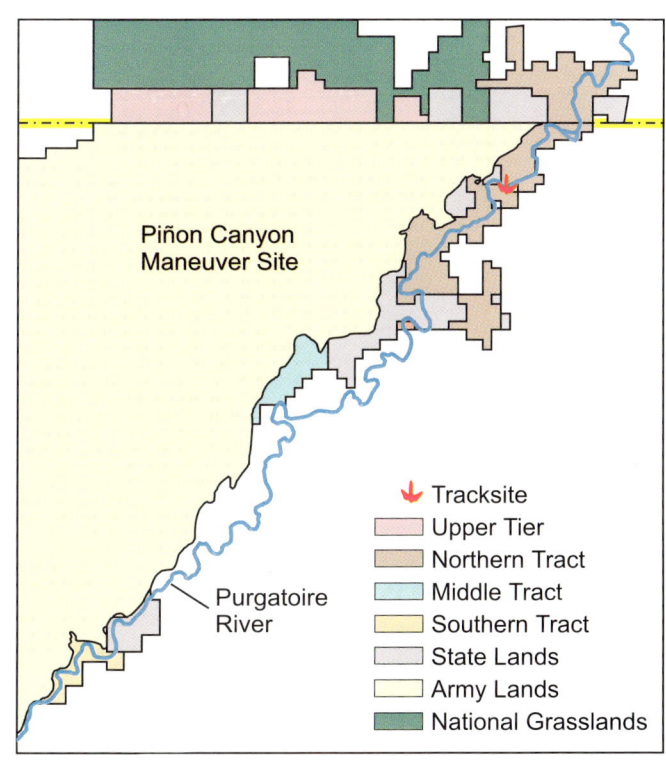

Piñon Canyon Maneuver Site

Purgatoire River

↓ Tracksite
▭ Upper Tier
▭ Northern Tract
▭ Middle Tract
▭ Southern Tract
▭ State Lands
▭ Army Lands
▭ National Grasslands

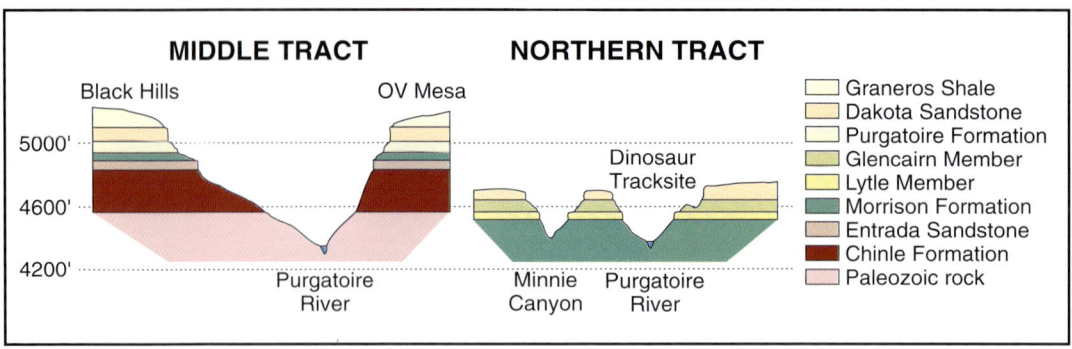

MIDDLE TRACT

NORTHERN TRACT

Black Hills

OV Mesa

Dinosaur Tracksite

5000'

4600'

4200'

Purgatoire River

Minnie Canyon

Purgatoire River

- Graneros Shale
- Dakota Sandstone
- Purgatoire Formation
- Glencairn Member
- Lytle Member
- Morrison Formation
- Entrada Sandstone
- Chinle Formation
- Paleozoic rock

Cross-section of strata showing the geologic variation of the Middle and Northern Tracts.

Geological map of the rocks exposed in the area.

basal portions of the canyon walls are composed of the Jurassic Morrison Formation. Quaternary sand and gravel river deposits (alluvium) are found along the margins of the river channel, forming incised earthy banks. The upper portion of the canyon walls is composed of rocks of the Purgatoire and Dakota Formations. The Purgatoire consists of two subunits called the Lytle and Glencairn Members. The lowest prominent cliff in the canyon wall is represented by sandstones of the light buff-colored Lytle Member of the Purgatoire Formation. Blocks of Lytle sandstone slump down the slopes, often obscuring the base of the formation. The Glencairn Member consists of marine shale and forms the greyish-colored slope between the Lytle Member and the overlying, orange-brown Dakota Sandstone Formation that forms the cliffs at the top of the canyon. Throughout the area the Dakota Sandstone is overlain by another marine deposit, the Graneros Shale, which is less resistant and forms the gentle topography on the prairie away from the canyon rim. The Morrison Formation and the Lytle Member of the Purgatoire Formation are nonmarine deposits that yield terrestrial plant fossils, dinosaur bones and tracks, and fresh water invertebrates such as snails and clams. West of

Tracksite

Purgatoire River

- Fort Hays
- Carlile/Greenhorn/ Graneros
- Dakota/Purgatoire
- Morrison/Ralston Creek/ Entrada
- Triassic Rock
- Permian Rock

the Rocky Mountains, the Morrison Formation is divided into two members. The lower, sandy Salt Wash Member and the upper, shaley and silty Brushy Basin Member. In the Canyonlands, and east of the Rockies, geologists can not distinguish these members and so refer to the Morrison as "undifferentiated." The overlying units are marine or marginal marine (coastal) deposits that contain typical marine invertebrates such as oysters, ammonites, fish, and various burrows and trails.

GEOLOGIC HISTORY

During the Permian Period (290- to 245-million years ago), much of Colorado was a low-lying region, where desert conditions prevailed. In eastern Colorado, a shallow sea had gradually dried up, leaving thin limestone and gypsum beds along its margin. These strata (layers of rock) are known as the Big Basin, Dry Creek, and White Horse Formations and are devoid of fossils. The western shore of the sea was characterized by beaches and sand dunes, preserved along the Colorado Front Range as the Lyons Sandstone. During part of the Permian, a shallow sea extended from Idaho, Utah, and Wyoming into northwestern Colorado. At the end of the Permian Period, land plants and land vertebrates were well established, but few fossil remains have been found in Paleozoic rocks except for tracks of early reptiles and spiders in the Lyons Sandstone.

The first period in the Mesozoic Era was the Triassic (245- to 208-million years ago). In southeastern Colorado, deposits from this period are known as the Chinle Group—formerly called the Dockum Group—and are famous in Arizona for the Petrified Forest and Painted Desert scenery. A few early dinosaur tracks are found in these strata just north of the Oklahoma state line.

The second period in the Mesozoic Era was the Jurassic (208- to 144-million years ago) when dinosaurs were most prevalent throughout the world. In the Purgatoire Tracksite area, Jurassic deposits include the Entrada Sandstone, Ralston Creek/Bell Ranch Formation, and the Morrison Formation. The Entrada Sandstone is a wind deposited formation of fossil sand dunes and is not known to contain fossils here, but a small crocodilian fossil has been found in the formation in Utah.

Overlying the Entrada Formation are rocks equivalent to the Ralston Creek Formation (of southeastern Colorado) and the Bell Ranch Formation (of northeastern New Mexico). These rocks represent arid coastal lagoons associated with shallow seaways.

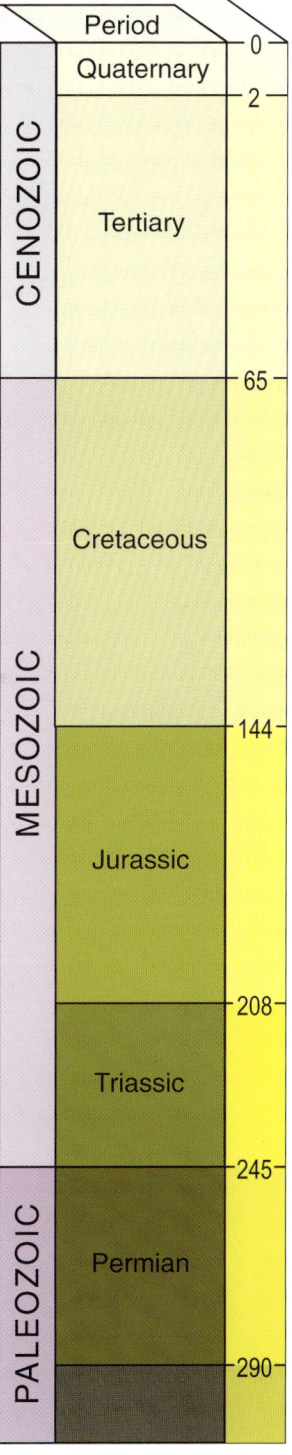

Geologic timeline.

These rocks are often gypsum-bearing and soils developed from them have high salinity. Conglomerates at the base of the unit contain both vertebrate body fossils (bones) and plant fossils, which are rare in Middle Jurassic rocks in the United States. Tracks have also been found in the Bell Ranch Formation in the Dry Cimarron Valley in northeastern New Mexico and are similar to tracks found in strata of the same age in Utah. There have also been reports of pterosaur tracks at about this level in rocks in Oklahoma. This is consistent with the evidence of a shallow seaway extending into the area, because pterosaurs inhabited marine shoreline areas.

Geologists studying this area in the 20th century have failed to agree on the naming of Triassic and Jurassic rocks that make up the sequence below the Morrison. For example, one recent suggestion indicates that the Entrada may have been misidentified and confused with a Triassic wind blown deposit known as the Jelm. Similarly, there is controversy and confusion over the age and naming of strata referred to here as the Ralston Creek/Bell Ranch Formation. Much of the uncertainty comes from the lack of useful fossils that can help determine the age of the rocks and the relatively small area of rock exposures in the canyonlands. We look forward to discovering further fossils and footprints that will shed light on the Mesozoic history of the Canyonlands prior to Morrison time.

The Morrison Formation of Late Jurassic age (about 162- to 144-million years ago) overlies the Ralston Creek/Bell Ranch Formation. The lower half of the Morrison consists of rocks deposited in lakes (lacustrine deposits) and the upper half comprises those deposited by rivers (fluvial deposits). The Morrison Formation consists of shales and sandstones that represent floodplain environments and river channels; siltstones and shales that represent soil-forming environments; and limestone layers that represent lake or lacustrine environments. The formation is described in more detail in the "Description of the Tracksite" and "Results of Research on Dinosaur Tracks" sections of this book. In addition to containing the longest dinosaur trackway known in North America, the Morrison Formation has also produced dinosaur bones, both near and within the Purgatoire Tracksite area. A partial hind limb and foot of a sauropod has been found at the main track site. In 1992, Jim Herrell of La Junta and his brother, Kim Herrell of Castle Rock reported brontosaur bone fossils in the Morrison near the tracksite on private land. In addition, the Morrison Formation yields fish scale, invertebrate, and plant fossils.

The Cretaceous Period (144- to 65-million years ago) was the last period of the Mesozoic Era. During the middle of this period a vast sea began to move across Colorado from the southeast, and marine condi-tions eventually prevailed. This shallow inland sea is referred to as the

Cretaceous Western Interior Seaway. Cretaceous formations deposited include—from oldest to youngest—the Purgatoire, Dakota Sandstone, Graneros Shale, Greenhorn Limestone, Carlile Shale, and Niobrara. The Purgatoire Formation includes two members, the Lytle and the Glencairn.

The Lytle Member consists of fluvial sandstone and conglomerate and is Early Cretaceous in age. The Lytle represents a high-energy fluvial or river environment and is therefore unlikely to produce many fossils, although some fossil wood has been found. The Glencairn Member consists of relatively thin sandstone and marine shale beds. The sandstone beds contain burrows and trails of invertebrates and represent deposition in fluvial and coastal environments during Early Cretaceous time. The marine shale beds, which contain a sparse assortment of oyster and burrow fossils, represent a shallow and marginal-marine environment indicating the presence of marine deposits from this interior seaway. The Glencairn forms the slope between the lower, ledge-forming sandstones of the Lytle and the overlying brown Dakota sandstone forming the rimrock of the canyon.

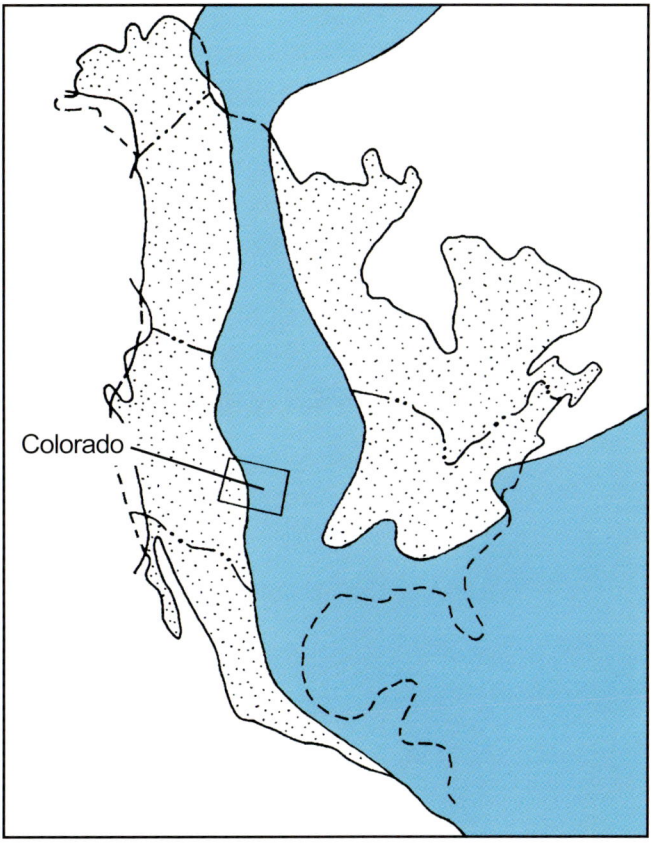

Map showing the extent of the Cretaceous Western Interior Seaway.

The Dakota Sandstone Formation is of fluvial and shallow-marine origin and forms the prominent sandstone cliffs that cap the canyon walls. The rocks contain very abundant burrows and invertebrate traces. Iguanodon-like dinosaur tracks are abundant in this unit from northeastern New Mexico to Boulder, Colorado. Tracks of crocodiles are known in the area as well. The sheer abundance of dinosaur tracks has led to the concept of a "Dinosaur Freeway"—a sequence of track-bearing rocks that extend over a huge area and represent the trampled shoreline of the Cretaceous Interior Seaway. It may also represent a dinosaur migration route. The Cretaceous Dinosaur Freeway should not be confused with the Jurassic Purgatoire Tracksite, which is 50-million years older and represents an entirely different dinosaur community.

The overlying shales and limestones of the Graneros Shale, Greenhorn Limestone, Carlile Shale, and Niobrara Formations are Late

Cretaceous in age and represent marine deposition. They contain invertebrate fossils in the Purgatoire Tracksite area and form the slopes and low rounded hills above the canyon rim.

There are no rocks in this area that represent the Tertiary Period (65- to 2-million years ago) or the "Age of Mammals." However, sands and gravels were deposited in the valley bottom during the Quaternary Period (2-million years ago to present), during a time when the Earth was experiencing the last ice age. These deposits contain vertebrate fossils of mammoth, bison, and other mammals.

CULTURAL HISTORY OF THE AREA

The Purgatoire Valley has an abundant and fascinating history and many historical resources. The area also contains a rich record of prehistoric culture including abandoned settlements, rock houses and shelters, and rock art.

The prehistory of the Purgatoire area is based on studies of a wider area that encompasses southeastern Colorado, western Oklahoma, Texas, northeastern New Mexico, the Central Plains, and the Southwest. Southeastern Colorado is thought to be a transitional zone between cultures of the American Southwest and the Great Plains. This leads to overlapping, and sometimes hard to identify, mixes of artifacts and architecture.

The earliest generally accepted evidence of human occupation in southeastern Colorado is from the Paleo-Indian Period (10,000 B.C. to 5500 B.C.). Early in this period—at the end of the last ice age—small bands of nomadic hunter-gatherers called the Clovis hunted large game animals such as mammoth, camel, horses, and others. The Folsom culture overlaps and follows the Clovis. The climate was gradually warming, and many of the large game animals became extinct. The foraging people adjusted to the available resources, turning to animals such as

A hunter-gatherer scouting for possible prey.

pronghorns, hares, wolves, an extinct type of bison, and others to survive. Both the Clovis and the Folsom are known for their distinctive fluted projectile points. Although some surface points have been found in the area, no intact sites for either culture has been reported in southeastern Colorado.

Following the Folsom was the Plano culture. Fluting of points was discontinued, and fine flaked points appeared. An increasingly more organized social structure was marked by more varied tools, well-organized hunting parties, and evidence of religious practice. The presence of milling stones indicates that there was also more emphasis on the processing of plant foods. There is much evidence of Plano culture in the area, but few intact sites.

During the Archaic Period (approximately 5500 B.C. to A.D. 200) people still followed a hunter-gatherer lifestyle, hunting whatever game was available and gathering wild plants. Tools for plant processing improved and there were further variations in projectile point styles and techniques, including notching. Plant fibers began to be used for the construction of coiled baskets and cording for lines and nets. The Archaic way of life lasted for more than 6,000 years—the longest existing in Colorado, and probably in the New World. There are many Archaic sites in southeastern Colorado, most dating from late in the period. Rockshelters, living floors, crude barrier walls, and hearths have been found—some dating as early as 1550 B.C.

Around A.D. 200 a period known as the Ceramic began, continuing until A.D. 1750. The most significant developments of this period are the use of pottery and the development of the bow-and-arrow. Cultures in other parts of Colorado, such as the Anasazi and the Fremont were beginning to develop a communal, sedentary lifestyle utilizing horticulture. Southeastern Colorado peoples, however, remained semi-nomadic and continued to hunt and gather during the early part of this period. They did begin to make pottery at this time, a skill probably passed by travel along the river drainages from their eastern neighbors.

As the Ceramic Period developed, small masonry structures appeared in substantial numbers in southeastern Colorado, along with rock art and the beginnings of maize, beans, and squash agriculture to supplement hunting. This mixed farming and hunting culture is known as Apishapa and dates from about A.D. 1000. Many sites are located in defensible positions, on promontories or adjacent to river bottoms. Tools, ceramics, and

The area contains many petroglyphs (rock art).

architecture continued to improve, their styles indicating a variety of influences from surrounding areas, mostly the Plains. Late in the period, approximately A.D. 1300, sites declined sharply—possibly denoting warfare or drought. Earth rings and spaced stone rings called "tipi rings" began to appear, probably attributed to the beginning of the Apachean influence. The Apache were an Athabaskan-speaking people who began to migrate from the north into the area at this time. It was also during this time that the first contact with non-native people occured in the Plains. European trade goods such as iron, brass, and glass beads are found at sites of this period, along with indigenous trade of pottery and materials from different surrounding native cultures.

One culture specific to the Purgatoire area is called the Upper Purgatoire Complex. It reflects influences from the Puebloan Southwest and is characterized by semi-sedentary settlements, hunting and gathering, and floodplain farming. Houses of stone, adobe, and jacal (close-set wooden stakes plastered with mud), as well as bell-shaped storage pits and early pithouses, can be found in the area. This was an indigenous population that probably had contact with—but were completely separate from—the Anasazi. Ceramics show that trade with both the Plains and the Southwest occurred.

It was into this setting of mixed native cultures that the first Spanish explorers came to the Purgatoire Valley. At this time the Purgatoire Valley environment was a river oasis, lush and teeming with

Historic painting of the Purgatoire Valley. Courtesy, Colorado Historical Society.

life. When the Europeans arrived in the 1500s, they brought with them Old World diseases such as smallpox, which may have decimated the native populations of the area, leading to the withdrawal of the Puebloan-like culture. The Jicarilla Apache was the next significant culture to inhabit the area. Often called the "Apache Century," the period between 1620 and 1720 saw the Purgatoire Valley dominated by these people. Horses provided by trade with the Spanish gave the Apache military superiority over other tribes. The Apache hunted and farmed the valley, making the most of abundant natural resources. They welcomed others, such as the Navajo, to hunt the big game that migrated through the area. They believed that the Purgatoire River was a sacred stream, placed there by the Creator.

The "Lost Souls" of the Purgatoire.

The Arkansas River was then the border between what was politically Spain's New World empire and French Louisiana—however, the Spanish mostly ignored this northern area and did not seriously try to colonize. The Spanish colony of New Mexico had been established in 1598. It was sometime after this that a story is told of Spanish military explorers that ventured into the Purgatoire Valley in search of a route from New Mexico to Florida. The story tells that the Spaniards travelled with much gold to pay off soldiers in Florida upon their arrival. The regiment was never seen or heard from again. This led to the naming of the river—*El Rio de las Animas Perdidas en Purgatorio* or the River of Lost Souls in Purgatory. Many Spaniard's felt that the soldiers' souls were lost because they died without the benefit of clergy. A later account by an Indian native told that the regiment had been surrounded by Indians and a fight had occurred until no Spaniard was left living. Later French travellers referred to the river as the *Purgatoire* (pronounced Pur-ga-twa)—from the Spanish name—but also referred to it as the *Piquer l'Eau* or Water of Suffering. Another version for the origin of the river's name may come from the native peoples calling it the Spirit River—thought to be because the water disappeared into the ground and reappeared further down the canyon. While underground, the water made noises, making it seem as though inhabited by spirits. When other Americans travelled into the area, they supposedly had trouble with the French pronunciation, and the river became known as the "Picket Wire."

The 1700s saw the Comanches move in and push the Apache—and their lifestyle—to the south. The Comanche had obtained firearms

Historical map of the area showing the rivers, trails, and the location of native and non-native settlements. Courtesy, Colorado Historical Society.

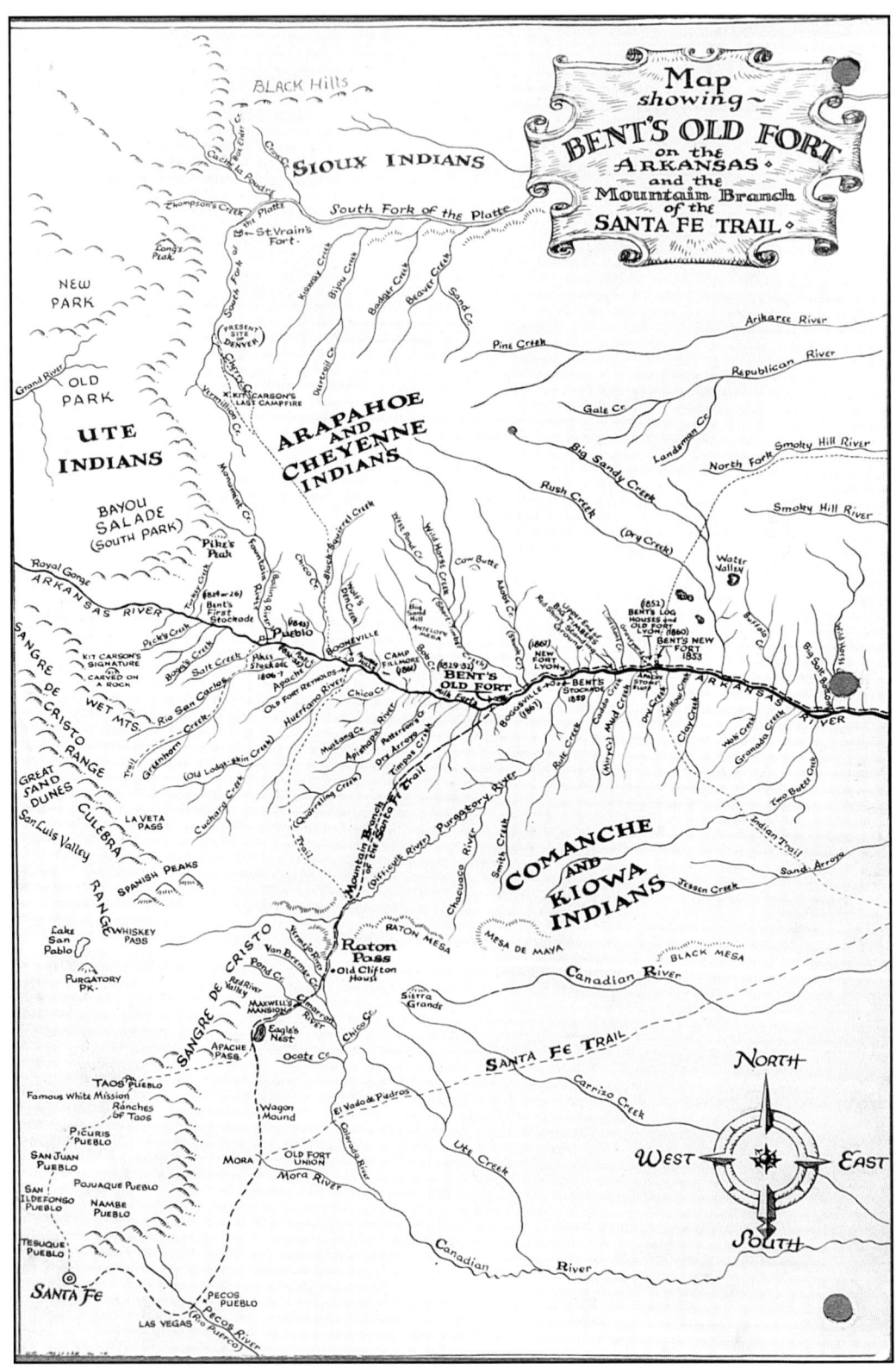

from French traders, giving them supremacy over the horse and lance that had been so successful for their predecessors. Trade with the Comanche allowed the French to establish a trade route from Louisiana to New Mexico by eliminating the Apache resistance in the area. The increasing trade and trapping in the area also brought a change in the environment of the Purgatoire Valley. Trapping denuded the area of the beaver and their dams that created the pools and marshes of the river oasis. As the beaver gradually disappeared, the streams of the valley became the ephemeral ones of today.

In the early 1800s the Louisiana Territories were acquired by the United States. The Arkansas River became the boundary between the peoples of the Northern and Southern Plains—Arapaho and Cheyenne moved in north of the Arkansas River, and the Comanche, Kiowa, and Kiowa-Apache moved to the south.

When Mexico won its independence from Spain in 1821, the Santa Fe trade route was opened. In 1826, four brothers named Bent and their partner Ceran St.Vrain, established a trading post on the northern bank of the Arkansas River. One story relates how the Bent brothers met a party of Cheyenne while camping in the area. The Cheyenne Yellow Wolf suggested that the Bents build a post near the river where he would bring his band and others to trade. The Bent's existing post—between Pueblo and Canon City—was too far from the buffalo range for good trade. The new post, which later was constructed into a fort, was to dominate trade in the area for more than 20 years. Bent's Fort, as it became known, was constructed between 1828 and 1832. The long construction time was due to William Bent's determination that it be made of the more durable and fireproof material adobe, instead of the more common log construction of the area. It was described in 1839 by a traveller as having an "outer wall...built of imperfectly burnt brick" while "on two sides arise two

A trapper from early in Colorado's history.

Historic artwork of activity at Bent's Fort. Courtesy, Colorado Historical Society.

William Bent, builder of Bent's Fort.

Ceran St. Vrain, a partner in business with the Bent brothers.

Charles Bent, older brother to William. Later the first U.S. governor of New Mexico.

Photos: courtesy, Colorado Historical Society.

little towers with loop holes" (for guns) and having an "ample court yard." This visitor was glad of the welcome, protection, and comfort offered by the fort so far from "civilization." Bent's Fort became the center of activity for trappers, traders, indigenous natives, Mexicans, government troops, and others who sought adventure in the area.

The Bents promoted peace among the various native tribes. Warfare was bad for business—good trade relations with their neighbors was essential. William Bent married Owl Woman, the daughter of a powerful Cheyenne priest. When she died in childbirth, he married her sister, Yellow Woman. Stories tell that William would travel or camp with his wife's people when he could get away from his responsibilities at the fort. The Bents were influential in the native community of the area and were concerned with political situations involving the tribes. Traders like William Bent knew and understood the native people and their ways and tried to intervene in treaty disputes and later conflicts.

After Mexico gained independence, the territorial governor granted lands to colonists in an effort to populate the northern border and prevent U.S. expansion. St. Vrain and others were granted up to four million acres—most of southeastern Colorado. The war with Mexico commenced at the height of Bent's Fort prosperity in 1846. With the fort on the north side of the river, and on American soil, it easily became a strategic location for the U.S. Army. William Bent was made a colonel for his assistance to the army during this time. When the army captured Santa Fe, it appointed William's brother Charles as the first American governor of New Mexico. His position was short-lived, however, as he was assassinated by Pueblo Indians and Mexicans in the 1847 Taos massacre. When peace came in 1848, the fort was once again a trading post. The area was opened to emigrants, bringing disease and wiping out much of the indigenous population. The disillusioned William dissolved the company and departed Bent's Fort with his family to a new location further along the Arkansas River. There, in 1854, he built a new Fort Bent—very similar to the old one but smaller. This fort was later renamed Fort Wise and later again renamed Fort Lyons. William Bent died of pneumonia in 1869.

From the time of Coronado's travels in 1541 through the time of the gold rush in 1859, the area was visited by non-native Americans but not permanently settled by them. Throughout the various political changes the area remained in the hands of the indigenous inhabitants until the gold rush. Bent's Old Fort was left to decay. In the 1850s the gold rush brought people streaming into Colorado. The 1860s brought Hispanic emigrants back into the area. The Dolores Mission and Cemetery are one record of their settlement efforts along the Purgatoire River. In 1871, a homesteader named Damacio Lopez led his,

and 11 other families to the mouth of Minnie Canyon. There they established a poor, but close-knit community. Accounts by Damacio's son Elfido, tell of the hard work and few tools these settlers had to dig ditches to irrigate their fields and produce crops.

The ruins of the Dolores Mission and Cemetery (above and below).

The settlement traded their produce with other villages along the Purgatoire River. The community continued to develop and by the 1880s, Damacio was serving as postmaster for this community of Bent Canyon, along with his own store and livestock. The Lopez family was one of the longest to stay in the area—remaining for two generations. Elfido eventually had his own homestead on the rim rock of the east side of the river canyon. Descendants of Elfido still live in the area.

By the time of the Civil War, unnecessary and avoidable conflicts between the army and the indigenous people developed, leading to the relocation of the native peoples. By the turn of the century, open-range livestock dominated the area, the Anglo-owned cattle ranches displacing the settlers. The Rourke family established a ranch on the Purgatoire River during this time. Growing from its original 40 acre settlement to over 52,000

acres, the ranch was one of the oldest and most successful in southeastern Colorado. Farming, mining, railroads, and urban industrial development soon followed. By early in the 1900s the land was opened for dryland farming homesteaders.

The large influx of people and use of the land destroyed much of the natural resources of the area, causing pollution and erosion that led to the formation of the arroyos that are now common in the valley. An early observer commented that Bent's Old Fort was still in fair condition when they arrived—it was gradually destroyed by the settlers taking the bricks away to build their homes and barns. Bent's Old Fort was declared a Registered National Historic Landmark in 1960 and has since been restored to its original appearance.

The restored Bent's Fort of today. Photo by Jack Rathbone.

The trail running parallel to the Purgatoire River has been used for transportation purposes from prehistoric times. The indigenous peoples of the area, Spanish explorers, Mexican traders and settlers, French and American trappers and merchants all used the trail extensively. The first "official" U.S. government expedition into the area in the 1820s noted that the trail was well used long before their presence. By the 1840s the trail was called Bent's Fort Road—later known as the Mountain Branch of the Santa Fe Trail. Purgatoire Valley has seen considerable migration and travel throughout the ages. The discovery of dinosaur trackways shows just how long the area has been inhabited.

HISTORY OF DISCOVERY
AND RESEARCH
ON DINOSAUR TRACKS

The Purgatoire Tracksite has an interesting but little-known scientific history. The first dinosaur tracking expedition to the Purgatoire Valley was initiated by Betty Jo Riddenoure, a schoolgirl from Higbee, some 12 miles downstream from the site. Although credited in the first newspaper report as the discoverer of the tracks, she declined to take credit, writing instead that her father Lawrence "Cuddle" Riddenoure and Ralph Owen, the district hydrographer, "found the tracks in August of 1935." The tracks were found in a limestone layer that spanned the river bed and were evidently known to local residents as early as the 1920s. The site was called "Rock Crossing," or in some reports "Elephant Crossing." Nevertheless, it was Betty Jo who told her science teacher, Don Hayes, about the tracks and this initiated the first documented expedition to the site in February of 1936. Initial newspaper reports were very misleading because they interpreted the track-makers as *Tyrannosaurus* and *Triceratops*—two Cretaceous dinosaurs that did not exist until almost 80-million years after the tracks were made.

News of the site soon spread beyond the local community. John Stewart MacClary, a local writer from Pueblo, wrote to Betty Jo that if she "did not discover the tracks in stone...well, neither did Columbus discover America." She indeed brought the site to the attention of the

Newpaper clipping of Betty Jo's find.

Looking somewhat like a crater, or perhaps a shallow stone dishpan, at the left foreground can be seen a track of a Triceratops, or forerunner of the modern Rhinoceros. Each track is about two feet

world, and in one of her several letters to MacClary, wrote "My first impressions...were that the tracks looked like a large turkey or bird had walked across the river."

After reading Betty Jo's accounts of her experiences, MacClary instigated a trip to the site (see box on page 24). MacClary's friends brought back photographs and information that inspired him to a flurry of investigative "mystery solving" through correspondence with the Colorado Museum of Natural History and the American Museum of Natural History. Through these letters MacClary established enough information to write short illustrated notes and letters for Life magazine (1936), Scientific American (1938), and Natural History (1939). He generated enough interest to entice Roland T. Bird, who assisted Barnum Brown, an American Museum paleontologist, to visit the site in November of 1938. Bird can be considered the first real dinosaur tracker to visit the Purgatoire Tracksite, and from his observations it is clear that he believed that the large rounded tracks were probably made by brontosaurs. This interpretation was correct—the Purgatoire Tracksite had revealed the first sauropod tracks ever reported. Bird's reluctance to

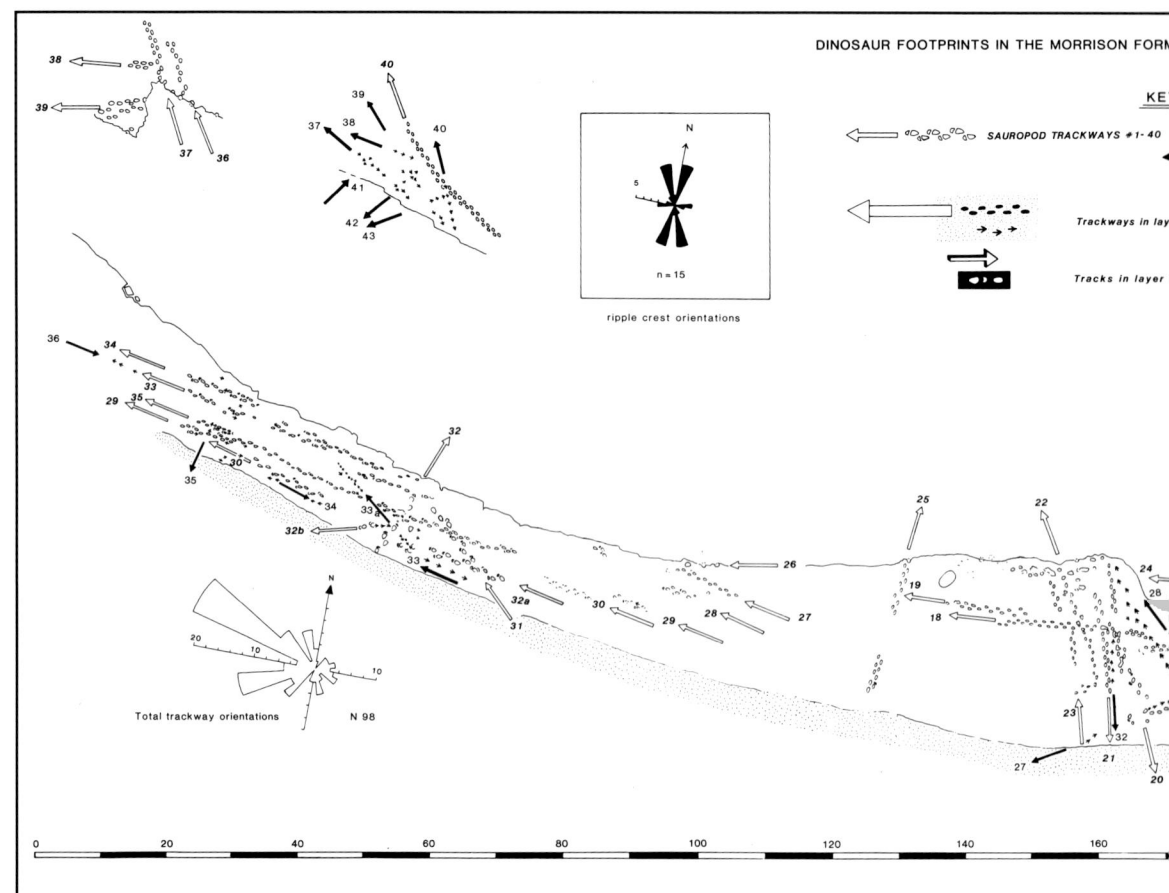

describe these in detail was the result of the discovery soon after of bigger and better sauropod tracks from Cretaceous-aged sites in Texas.

So it was, in November of 1938, while en route from New Mexico to a tracksite in Texas, Roland Bird made a special detour to see MacClary and visit the Purgatoire Tracksite. In doing so he joined MacClary in recording the first brontosaur tracks ever discovered. Although the written record is sparse and overshadowed by his reports of the second brontosaur tracksite discovery made in Texas a few days later, Bird wrote a short letter for Natural History magazine indicating that he was aware that the tracks might be attributed to brontosaurs. His exact words were: "We had first considered them possible sauropod tracks."

Largely because of the Texas dinosaur track discoveries—in more convenient and accessible locations—the Purgatoire Tracksite was all but forgotten. It was not until the early 1980s that it came to the attention of researchers at the University of Colorado at Denver and was studied seriously. This study was concluded in 1985, exactly 50 years after the first report. The first substantial paper was published in 1986, marking the 50th anniversary of MacClary's initial letter in Life magazine. The

A complete map of the dinosaur trackways.

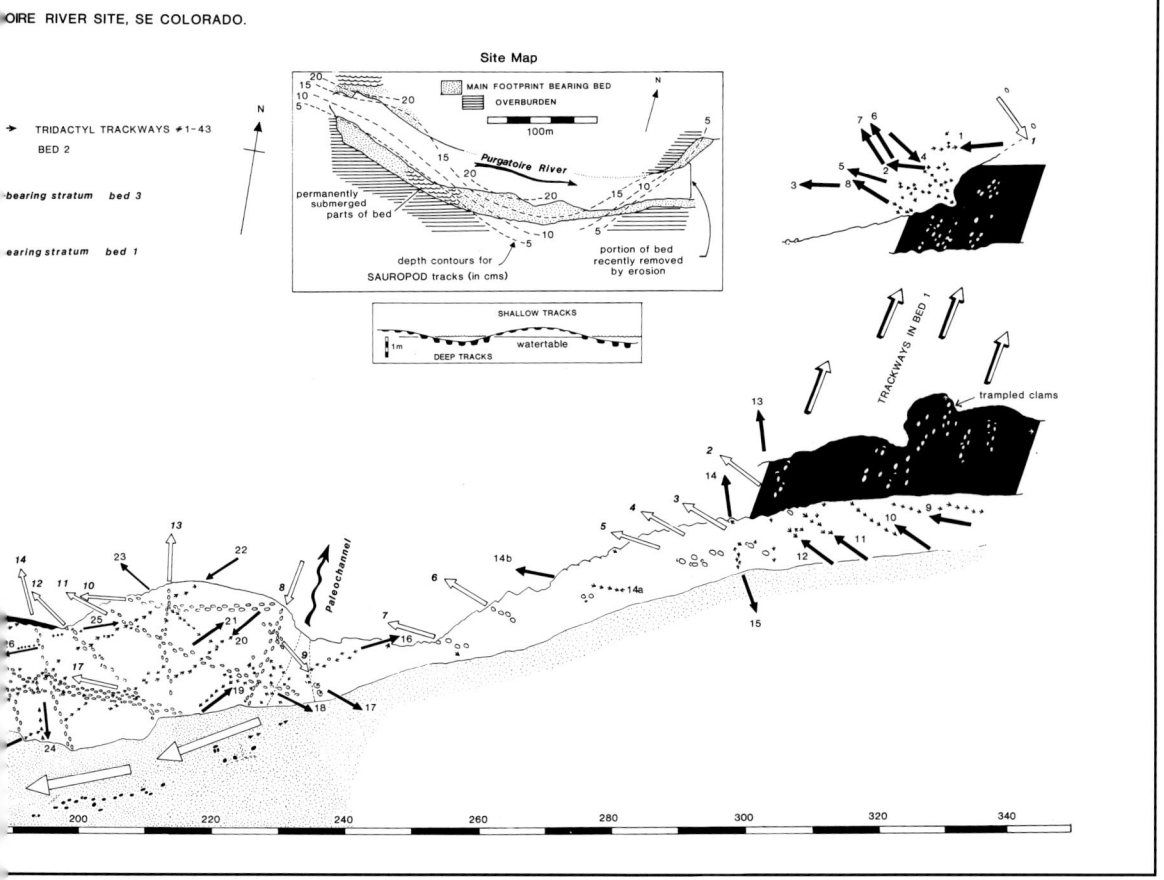

1986 publication included a complete map of the site revealing more than 1,300 tracks, representing trackways of about 100 different animals. Although this paper can be said to have "put the site on the map," it is not the complete story. There are a number of subsequent publications—including this one—stating new results and interpretations. More new contributions will no doubt be published in the future.

The First Dinosaur Tracking Expedition to the Purgatoire

MacClary was eager to investigate the tracks and with "the adventuring spirit of Huckleberry Finn...launched a motor expedition into the Purgatory badlands" with some "intimate friends...college men and women" that departed Pueblo, Colorado, on April 25, 1937. MacClary was an invalid and knew that his chance for "actually seeing the tracks-in-stone seemed very remote," then poignantly added "I did not go...one doesn't ford the Purgatory in a wheel-chair." His frustration, however, gave him "all the more reason for solving the mystery by remote control," and his records contain a detailed log of that April expedition. The group departed Pueblo at 9:15 a.m. and arrived in La Junta at 10:50, logging the mileage and precise time at every town in between. A scrawled sketch map exists showing the route south from La Junta over the chalk escarpment, marked "calcite" and "down hill," and on through Minnie Canyon, a 30-mile route that can still be accurately traced today.

MacClary's journal map of the first tracking trip.

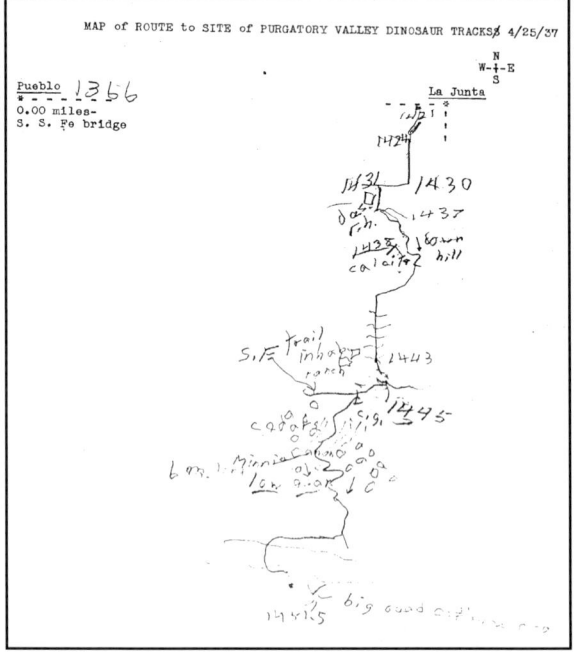

The Tracksite

A Jurassic Lake in southeastern Colorado

DESCRIPTION OF THE TRACKSITE

The Purgatoire Tracksite is associated with strata of the Morrison Formation, dating back to the Late Jurassic Epoch (about 162- to 144-million years ago). This epoch is sometimes known as the "Age of Brontosaurs" and falls close to the middle of the Mesozoic age of dinosaurs. The Morrison is world famous for having yielded the skeletal remains of some of the world's most well-known dinosaurs, including *Apatosaurus* (commonly called "Brontosaurus"), *Stegosaurus* (the Colorado State fossil), *Ultrasaurus* (the same as or very similar to *Brachiosaurus*, the world's largest dinosaur), *Allosaurus* (the most common carnivore from this epoch), and *Camptosaurus* (a large herbivorous ancestor of the duck-billed dinosaurs). In addition to these well-known large dinosaurs, the Morrison Formation has produced the remains of many other small vertebrates, including emu- and turkey-sized dinosaurs, turtles, pterosaurs, crocodiles, lizards, mouse-sized mammals, frogs, and fish. The Morrison has also produced fossils of clams, snails, crustaceans, and plants. In short, the Morrison Formation is one of the most productive fossil-bearing units in the western United States, and indeed the entire world.

Because the Morrison Formation is so fossilifer-ous, it has also been studied by geologists interested in understanding what types of ancient environments it represents. The general consensus is that the mixture of soft grey and purple shales interbedded with resistant brown and buff-colored sandstones represent floodplain environments and river channels. Many of these rocks are rich

Jurassic Period	Late	Age of Brontosaurs	
	Middle		
	Early		

in volcanic ash owing to extensive eruptions at that time. The grey-green and purple-red siltstones and shales represent fossil soils (known as paleosols), with the grey and green colors usually representing wetter conditions than the red-purple layers. Bones found in these deposits often represent the remains of smaller animals that were buried as the result of flooding into ponds and backwaters, whereas the sandstones often contain the remains of larger animals whose carcasses were robust enough to withstand the buffeting they received when washed along in the rivers. The Morrison also contains limestone layers, some formed in the soil (calcretes) and others formed in lakes (as at the Purgatoire Tracksite), but both representing relatively dry climatic conditions. The general consensus is that the Morrison Formation in this area reflects a seasonal, or semi-arid climatic regime similar to that of savannah regions in East Africa today. The presence of river and lake deposits proves that there was some water available—but the flora, fauna, and rock types suggest that water was often somewhat alkaline and in short supply.

HOW PALEONTOLOGISTS STUDY TRACKS

One of the first objectives of studying dinosaur tracks is to identify the trackmaker. In the modern world we can do this because we can observe animals making tracks. This is not the case with fossil footprints, because in most instances we are dealing with trackmakers that are extinct.

Tracking ancient beasts, therefore, requires different skills from modern tracking. Instead of waiting patiently for the trackmaker to show up, "trackers" (those who study tracks) must measure the size and shape of tracks and try to determine which fossil animal foot best matches the footprints. In some cases, paleontologists may have to study fossils from other regions where similarly-aged strata are known in order to find likely trackmakers. It may even prove impossible to find fossils of feet of the right age that match the track perfectly. When this happens, trackers can only go so far in narrowing down "who done it," and must conclude simply that it was an animal that to some degree was "similar" to a known fossil species.

This "best approximation" approach to identification of fossil footprints is reflected in the way tracks are named. Modern footprints are simply labelled according to their trackmakers, as in "mountain lion" tracks or "pigeon" tracks. In such cases we are identifying the species

A typical sauropod—or brontosaur—track.

or genus of a trackmaker very precisely. We can't do this with fossil footprints in most cases. We may recognize "brontosaur" tracks and distinguish them from tracks of carnivorous dinosaurs, but we cannot say which species or genus made a particular track. For this reason we are unable to talk confidently about tracks made by genus *Apatosaurus*, *Brachiosaurus*, or *Camarasaurus* in such a way as to imply that we can tell the difference. The best we can do is to label them all as sauropod—or brontosaur—tracks.

The track of a carnivorous theropod dinosaur.

Because trackers cannot usually label an *Apatosaurus* track with absolute certainty, an alternate system of names is used. Trackers use terms like *Brontopodus* (meaning "track of a brontosaur"). This implies that we know which family the trackmaker came from, but not the genus or species. These names are called "ichnogenus" (scientific classification for the track or trace) and are distinct from the genus and species names that are applied to the actual skeletal remains.

In practical terms, some field study is required before trackers can identify and interpret fossil footprints. Trackers collect basic information such as the size and shape of the tracks, the length of step and stride (a stride equals two steps), the depth of the tracks, and the direction of travel. Thorough trackers make a complete map of the site, trace the outlines of the best tracks, and create replicas of important specimens for museum reference collections. Making replicas of large dinosaur tracks can be quite a complicated and time-consuming activity involving considerable expense in materials and labor. First, a flexible rubber mold is made directly from the track impression in the rock. Second, a rigid support mold is made so the mold keeps its shape. Third, the rubber and support molds are taken back to the lab where they are used to make permanent replicas for research collections and museum exhibits. Such replicas can be made in plaster of paris or fiberglass.

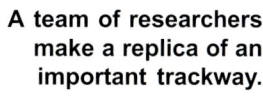

A team of researchers make a replica of an important trackway.

50 cm

Quadrupedal brontosaur tracks— _Brontopodus_.

Information that can be obtained from a trackway (below); a similar four-footed trackway (below right).

Tracks as Biologic Indicators

Tracks are the evidence of living animals and provide biological insights into the trackmaker's anatomy and behavior. First the tracks tell us: how big the animal was, how many toes it had, if it was a four-footed quadruped or a two-footed biped. These characteristics, along with the age of the strata, usually help us to identify the type of animal that made the tracks. This, however, is just the beginning of the biological evidence that can be gleaned from tracks.

When we have a trackway of consecutive footprints made by an individual animal, we can measure the width of the trackway to show if the animal walked erect, with one foot in front of the other, or semi-erect with a wide sprawling gait. We can also measure the step length, the direction in which the animal was heading, and use a simple formula to calculate the speed of the trackmaker.

In cases where we have trackways of several animals, we can use the tracks as a census of the ancient animal populations and communities that once inhabited the area. We can determine how many animals of a particular type lived in a given area, and whether they were small, large, or a mixture of various sizes. We can also learn if they were moving around randomly, or together as a herd or social group.

A count of each different type of trackmaker indicates which animals were common and which were rare. Though a single site tells

front foot
stride

step

trackway width

stride

us only about animal activity in a local area, in many cases we have several tracksites from a particular rock formation. This allows us to build a census of the animal community over a larger area and see if the same animals are consistently common or rare at a particular time.

Finally, when we find tracksites in several successive layers of strata, we can tell whether particular animal groups remained in the area for extended time periods, whether they increased or decreased in abundance, and when they appeared or disappeared. All this information gives us insight into the biology and ecology of the ancient animal communities, but is not the only information to be learned from tracks.

Tracks as Geologic Indicators

Tracks are also what geologists call sedimentary structures. When an animal steps in the sand or mud, it leaves a shallow track or a deep track depending on the consistency of the sediment. Therefore, tracks are indicators of the conditions underfoot. Paleontologists refer to tracks as "experiments in soil mechanics." Tracks are most commonly found along shorelines, where they often run parallel to the shoreline trend. This makes them valuable in reconstructing the ancient geography of a particular area. In the case of the Purgatoire Tracksite, many trackways trend westward along what were the shores of an ancient lake—a Jurassic Santa Fe Trail!

Unlike bones, which are sometimes washed into a sedimentary layer from miles away, tracks are always found in their original position. If we can correctly interpret the strata in which the tracks occur, we can understand the ancient environment in which the footprints were formed. Often we find evidence that tracks were made after a flood, or while a lake was drying out between

Bipedal theropod tracks—*Grallator*.

Trackway evidence from a two-legged carnivorous dinosaur (below); an actual trackway of this type (below left).

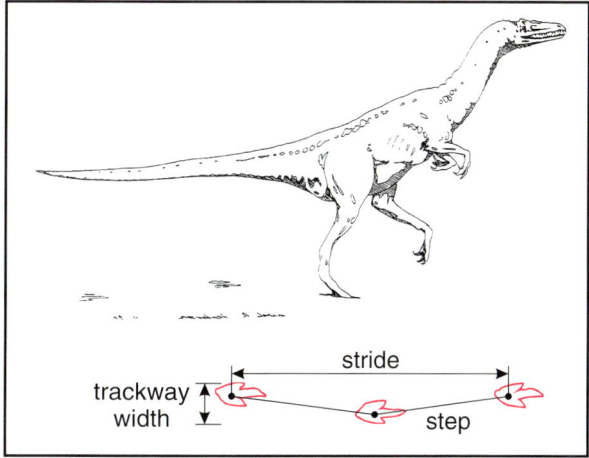

floods. We also often observe that a particular track type occurs only in a particular type of rock. This is evidence that certain animals preferred specific environments. Such evidence helps round out the picture of what life was like at the time. While they provide us with biological evidence of animal behavior and animal communities—they also furnish us with geological evidence about the ancient environment.

Results of Research on Dinosaur Tracks

As indicated above, dinosaur tracks provide many different types of information on trackmakers and the environments in which they lived. We can therefore summarize research results in a number of different categories. The obvious place to begin is with a description of the strata in which the tracks are found, because correct interpretation of these layers provides the key to understanding the trackmaker's environment.

Interpretation of the Track-bearing Layers at the Purgatoire Tracksite

Dinosaurs were part of the ancient environment, so to interpret tracks without interpreting the rocks in which they were found results in an incomplete study. It would be rather like a biologist describing the size, shape, and color of a plant or animal without saying whether it came from the ocean, desert, or rain forest.

First we must summarize what the rocks tell us about the ancient environment in which the tracks were made. All the sedimentary rock layers that contain tracks at the Purgatoire Tracksite indicate that the depositional environment was a lake basin—hence the name "Dinosaur Lake."

The track-bearing strata consist of alternating layers of tough, light grey limestone and soft, dark grey shale. The limestones are resistant to erosion and comprise the layers that make up the stream bed and prominent ledges along the banks at Rock Crossing—the local name for an old ford at the Purgatoire Tracksite. By contrast, the shales are easily crumbled and weathered, allowing the river to undercut the resistant beds and causing the limestone slabs to collapse into the river.

The limestones and shales represent an ancient lake environment. The shales clearly represent accumulations of mud in the lake itself when water levels were high, whereas the limestones represent accumulations of coarser, sand-textured sediment along the lake shore when water levels were lower. Evaporation of lake waters is indicated by the presence of limestone and certain salt crystals. The shales contain remains of fossilized algae, snails, and minute crustaceans known as "seed shrimp"

(ostracods) and "clam shrimp" (conchostrachans), all of which are typical of quiet water or low-energy, shallow lakes. Clam shrimp typically occur in areas with seasonal climates and distinct dry seasons. By contrast, the limestones contain impressions of large plant stems, scattered fish bones, trampled clams, dinosaur bones, and, of course, abundant tracks. The limestones also contain ripple marks caused by waves and tiny limey spheres known as ooids which are caused by the action of waves in shallow water. All of this evidence supports the conclusion that the limestones represent limey mudflats around the margins of the lake. The alternation of limestone and shale layers also indicates that the lake level fluctuated from time to time, quite possibly on a seasonal basis, but also on longer-term cycles of decades or centuries. The overall picture is one of a fair-sized lake, several tens of kilometers in diameter (10 kilometers is about 6 miles), with potable water most, if not all of the time. The lake was inhabited by a reasonably healthy flora and fauna of algae, snails, crustaceans, and fish. The lake margins were all or partly vegetated, locally inhabited by clams, and frequented by several different types of dinosaurs.

On the surface of the main track layer, there is evidence that tracks get deeper towards the north. By measuring the depth of the brontosaur tracks, one can produce a contour map suggesting that the shoreline trended from east to west. Further studies of the tracks indicate that most of the dinosaurs walked along this shoreline trend.

Tracks are found in all four of the main limestone layers identified at the site. In most cases, the tracks are moderately shallow and occur in the top of the limestone beds, indicating that the footprints were made at a dry time after lake levels had fallen somewhat. Other tracks are deeper and found at the base of limestone beds, indicating that they were made in wetter conditions when the water level was high.

Six Dinosaur Visits to "Dinosaur Lake"

Layers of strata represent slices of geologic time, usually decades, centuries, millennia, or even millions of years apart. The Purgatoire track beds provide an excellent example. Each of the four limestone layers represent a different episode in prehistory, even though they lie close together. In our initial study, we numbered the layers as beds 1 through 4. Further study reveals, however, that there are three track beds—or levels of track-making episodes—associated with bed 2. This makes a total of six track-bearing levels. What this boils down to is evidence of a minimum of six occasions when dinosaurs visited the lake.

Based on the number and type of tracks, the depth of the tracks, the orientation of the trackways, and the associated fossils, we will discuss each dinosaur visit and the environmental conditions existing on each occasion.

Each limestone track bed at the Purgatoire site represents different episodes from the past.

Dinosaur Visit One: Track bed 1 reveals abundant evidence of large brontosaurs and various smaller bipedal dinosaurs that trampled through a soft limey mud containing clams and primitive plants known as

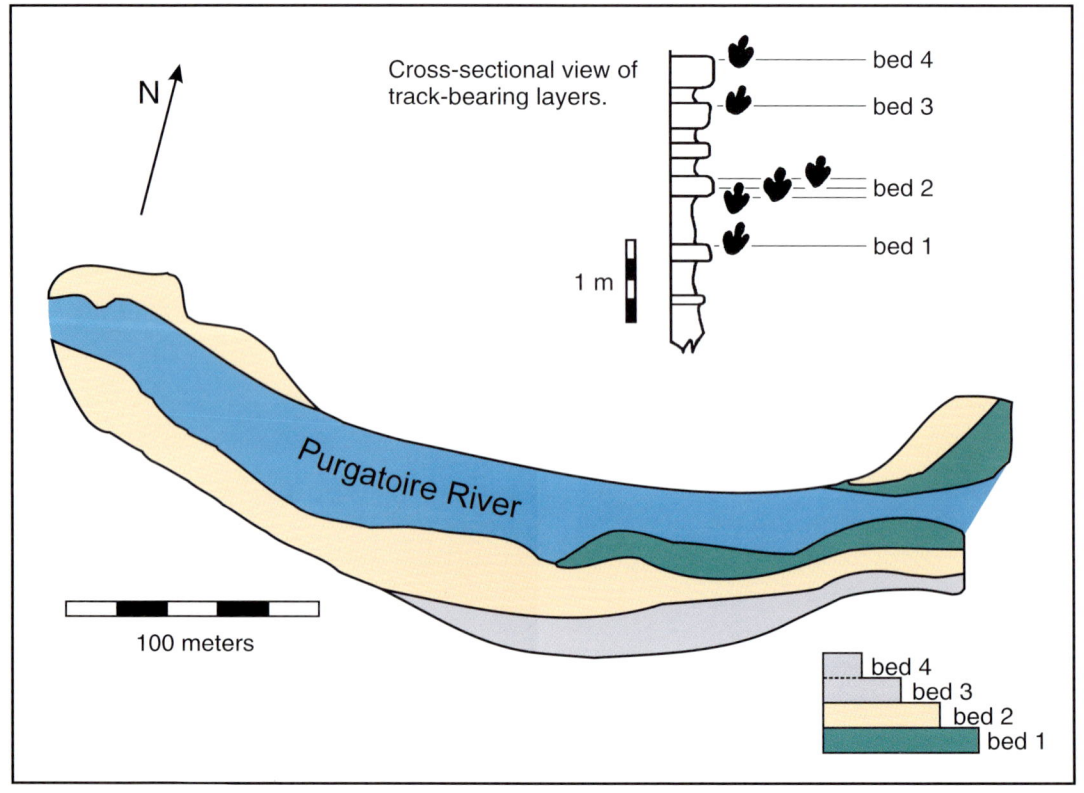

N

Cross-sectional view of track-bearing layers.

bed 4
bed 3
bed 2
bed 1

1 m

Purgatoire River

100 meters

bed 4
bed 3
bed 2
bed 1

horsetails. The extensiveness of the trampling indicates that there was a lot of dinosaur activity at this time.

Dinosaur Visit Two: At the bottom of limestone bed 2 we find deep footprints that were made before the limestone accumulated, and were then filled in by bed 2. This suggests that animals were wading in shallow, muddy parts of the lake, perhaps at some distance from the shore.

Dinosaur Visits Three and Four: There are two different footprint layers at the top of bed 2: one at the very top and one just below the surface. The lower one contains a few well-preserved tracks of small bipedal, carnivorous dinosaurs that were clearly made before the accumulation of the uppermost layers of this bed. The discovery of tracks within the layer, rather than just on top of it, provides insights into how bed 2 accumulated. Previously, interpretations had been that bed 2—which consists of sand-sized particles and exhibits distinctive ripple marks— was washed into place by a single storm or flood, or was deposited during a rapid change in lake level. The evidence of tracks within the layer argues against these ideas, and seems to suggest that the sand accumulated along the shoreline more gradually, during a time when dinosaurs walked along the shore.

In all studies to date, most attention has been focussed on the tracks in the upper surface of bed 2 (fourth track level), simply because this is where we find the most tracks. Bed 2 is by far the most resistant layer, thus providing the most extensive surface available for study. Photos published by Bird and MacClary indicate that this was also the case in the 1930s.

Dinosaur Visit Five: There are a few poorly preserved tracks associated with the top of bed 3. These are in a limestone layer containing fish remains and traces of plant roots.

Dinosaur Visit Six: The highest level so far recorded with tracks is limestone bed 4. This bed contains the remains of a sauropod skeleton that was damaged and disturbed by extensive trampling activity. The trampling activity was so intense, there are only a few clear tracks. Again, the trampling evidence suggests abundant dinosaur activity in the area.

Overall, the track evidence exhibited at these six different levels indicates that Dinosaur Lake was visited by dinosaurs repeatedly,

A deep footprint that was made before the limestone of bed 2 accumulated and filled in the impression.

The well-preserved track of a small bipedal, carnivorous theropod dinosaur.

and that on at least three occasions dinosaurs were probably present in large numbers. In the following sections we examine footprint evidence that allows us to: identify the types of trackmakers that were present; ascertain their movement in herds and aspects of their individual behavior, such as posture, locomotion, and speed; and propose certain ideas about the animal populations and ecology.

WHO DONE IT? IDENTIFYING THE TRACKMAKERS

First, we must describe and summarize the fossil footprint data. The most systematic way to do this is to count the number of trackways known from each level and assign them to the appropriate categories. In the case of the Purgatoire Tracksite, this is relatively easy to do. The tracks fall into only two broad categories. First, we have the large, slightly elephantine tracks of quadrupeds that were undoubtedly made by sauropods (brontosaurs), and second, we have a variety of three-toed tracks attributable to bipedal dinosaurs.

Brontosaur Tracks

Brontosaur trackways comprise two distinct types, wide-gauge and narrow-gauge. The best examples of wide-gauge types are footprints from the Cretaceous in Texas that were given the ichnospecies (species **The two distinct** classification for the track or trace) name *Brontopodus birdi*, named after **types of brontosaur** Roland T. Bird. Individual footprints from the Purgatoire Tracksite are **trackways.**

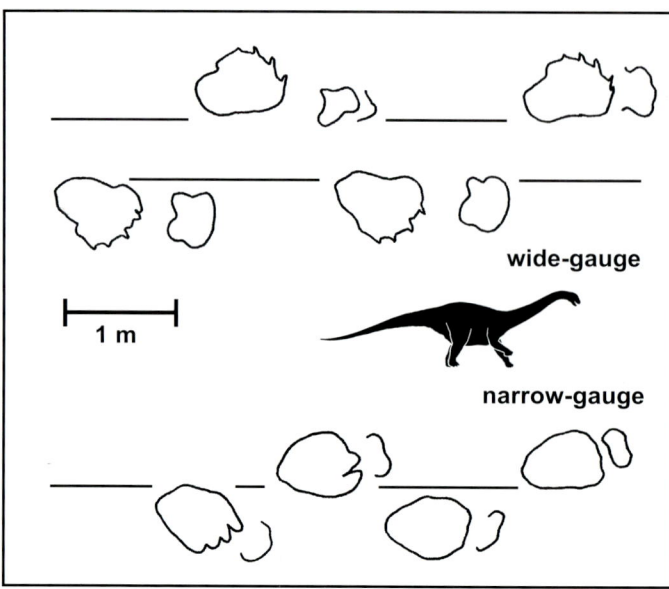

1 m

wide-gauge

narrow-gauge

narrow-gauge and though similar in general shape to the Texas tracks, they make up a different trackway pattern. Therefore, they can be given a different name, in this case, *Parabrontopodus* (meaning towards or similar to *Brontopodus*). Among the several dozen trackways at the Purgatoire Tracksite, we have identified a relatively large, broad-footed, narrow-gauge trackmaker and a relatively small, narrow-footed, narrow-gauge trackmaker, which we suggest may represent different dinosaur species.

Another possibility is that the tracks represent different age groups or different sexes within the same species.

When we compare the tracks with the skeletons of possible trackmakers, we enter the realm of speculation. The sauropod—or brontosaur—order, technically known as Order Sauropoda, contains:

- Various assorted types,
- The brachiosaurid family,
- The camarasaurid family, and
- The diplodocid family.

In all probability the difference between wide- and narrow-gauge trackways reflects different families of brontosaur trackmakers. However, this can not be proven at present, partly because of insufficient research on the posture and locomotion of sauropods. It has been suggested that wide-gauge trackways might have been made by brachiosaurids. If this is true, then this family was evidently not represented at the Purgatoire Tracksite. This seems reasonable because both camarasaurids (e.g. *Camarasaurus*) and diplodocids (e.g. *Diplodocus* and *Apatosaurus* otherwise known as "Brontosaurus") are much more common than brachiosaurids in the Morrison Formation.

Other Dinosaur Tracks

All non-brontosaur tracks at the Purgatoire Tracksite represent bipedal animals with three-toed footprints. Such tracks are usually attributed to carnivorous dinosaurs known as theropods or to the group of mainly bipedal herbivores known as ornithopods. Thus, at least two major groups of quadrupedal dinosaurs, the plated stegosaurs and the armored ankylosaurs—both of which are known from skeletal remains in the Morrison Formation—are evidently not represented at the site. In fact, tracks of these two groups are very rare from the Late Jurassic of North America.

The possible three-toed track-types at the Purgatoire site.

Trackers have traditionally found it difficult to decide whether particular types of three-toed tracks were made by theropods or ornithopods. This is because there is a lot of similarity or "convergence" between the feet of these two groups. Convergence results when different animals develop similar adaptations and morphology as exemplified by the wings of bats, which are mammals, and pterosaurs, which were reptiles. Theropod and ornithopod tracks are convergent with tracks made by birds, and were interpreted as those of ancient birds when first discovered.

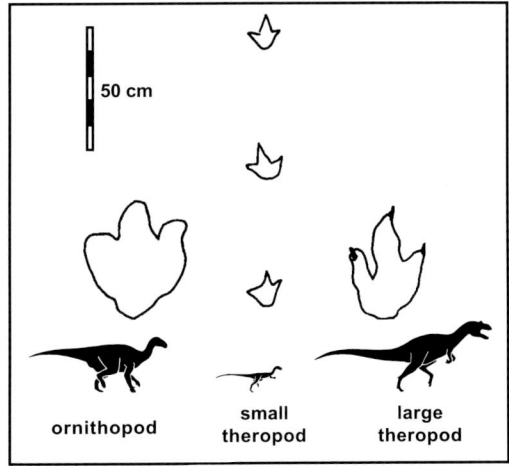

50 cm

ornithopod

small theropod

large theropod

The Purgatoire Tracksite is known for a number of different three-toed track types. They range in size from about 15 centimeters (6 inches) to about 45 centimeters (18 inches) in length. Such a range in size indicates a wide variety of trackmakers, from animals the size of a large turkey to a 9-meter (30-foot) allosaur weighing at least a ton. It is fairly easy to estimate the size of a dinosaur from its footprints. The rule of thumb for most bipedal dinosaurs is that the hip height equals about four to five times the foot length. Therefore, the Purgatoire animals ranged

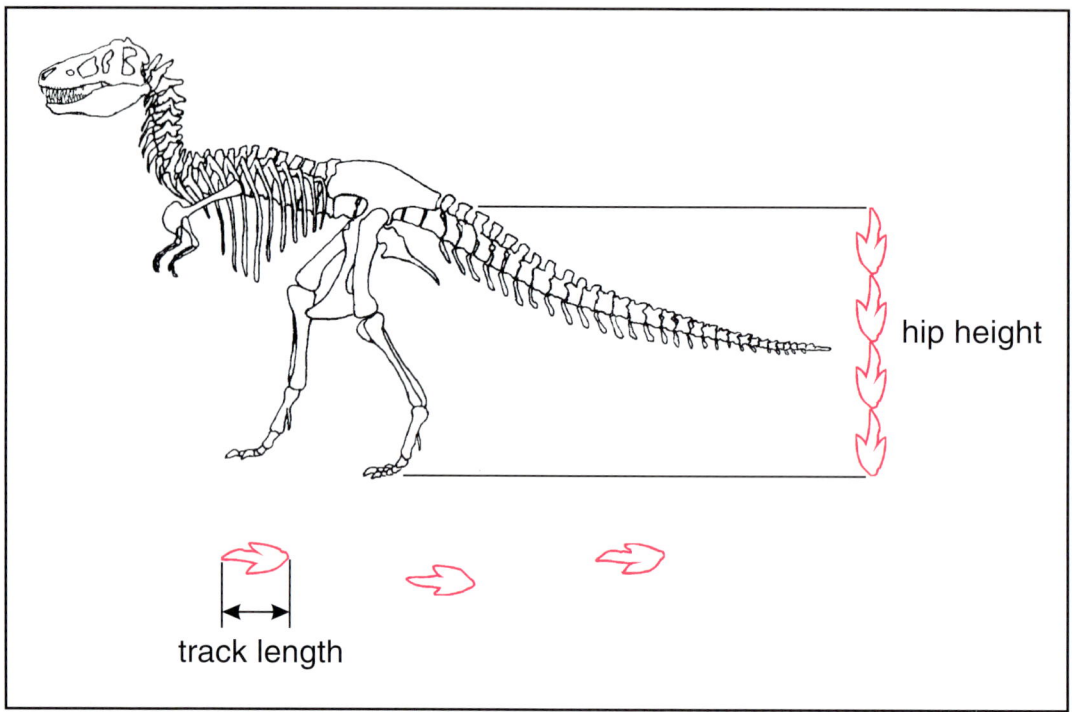

hip height

track length

An easy to remember rule is that the hip height is about four to five times the foot length.

from 0.6 to about 2.5 meters (2 to about 8 feet) at the hip. Knowing these size differences does not allow us to identify the trackmaking species precisely, but it does narrow the choices a little. For example, among the carnivorous dinosaurs that existed during Morrison time, *Allosaurus* and *Ceratosaurus* were two of the larger animals, and *Ornitholestes* was one of several diminutive forms.

Tracks of theropod dinosaurs are longer than they are wide. They may also show claw-marks.

Carnivore or Herbivore?

Because the two main groups of bipedal dinosaurs, the carnivores (or theropods) and the herbivores (or ornithopods) made very similar, three-

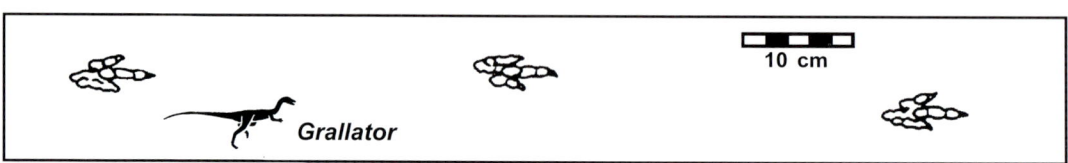

Grallator

10 cm

toed footprints, it can be difficult to distinguish between their tracks. Useful guidelines are:

- Tracks of carnivorous dinosaurs sometimes reveal sharp claw impressions. Their outline (shape) is also less symmetrical than that of ornithopod tracks.
- Tracks of carnivorous dinosaurs are usually greater in length than in width, whereas tracks of ornithopods are generally as long as they are wide.
- Carnivorous dinosaurs tended to take longer steps and made narrower trackways than ornithopods of the same size.
- Tracks of carnivorous dinosaurs are not as toed-in (pigeon-toed) as those of ornithopods in most cases.

Ornithopod tracks appear pigeon-toed and foot length and width are similar.

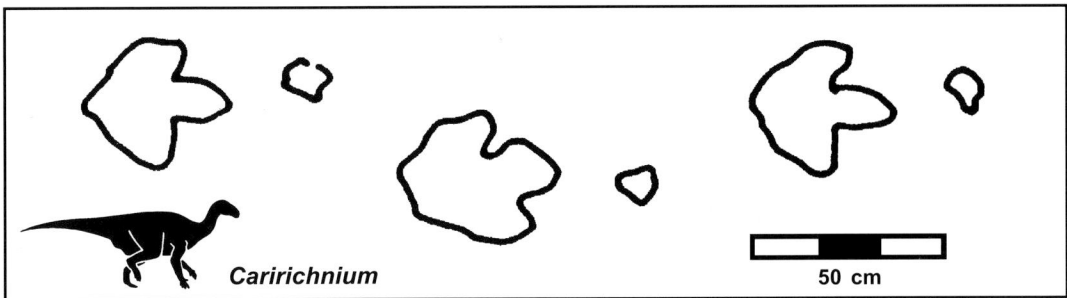

Caririchnium

50 cm

Although these general differences are not foolproof criteria for distinguishing trackmakers, they do provide useful guidelines. Based on these criteria we conclude that most, if not all, of the three-toed tracks from the Purgatoire Tracksite were made by theropods. This conclusion is slightly controversial because many feel that the three-toed trackmakers were ornithopods. Also, a dinosaur community with a large number of carnivores appears to be at variance with normal ecological principles. We will examine both aspects of these problems.

The Ornithopod Trackmaker Interpretation

The ornithopod trackmaker interpretation was first proposed by Charles Sternberg of the Canadian Geological Survey in a letter to MacClary dated February 8, 1939. In this letter Sternberg noted that "the outlines of the Purgatoire tracks are very similar to the ones I described from the Peace River in British Columbia." They were attributed by Sternberg to one of "the bipedal, herbivorous, dinosaurs similar to the Camptosaurs or Iguanodonts." These tracks—named *Gypsichnites*—are in turn similar to tracks described in 1899 by the famous dinosaur hunter Othniel C. Marsh from the Morrison Formation of South Dakota and attributed to camptosaurs. Roland Bird later underscored this interpretation in his article in the April 1939 issue of Natural History, when he wrote that "the

Gypsichnites as described by Sternberg in 1932. These tracks were attributed to camptosaurs.

three-toed prints apparently were made by one of the iguanodont dinosaurs."

Because no further work was done on the Purgatoire tracks between the 1930s and the 1980s, there was no reason to doubt the interpretations of Sternberg and Bird, both of whom were regarded as authorities on dinosaur tracks in the 1930s. Thus in 1986, when the first University of Colorado study was published, we "provisionally" agreed with the ornithopod (cf. *Camptosaurus*) interpretation on the basis of the small proportion (three or four percent) that show claw impressions. This interpretation seemed to make sense because predators are supposed to be rarer than prey (ratio about 1:30). Results of new studies in the 1980s made us realize that the ornithopod interpretation was doubtful or incorrect. In two papers published in 1988 and 1989, we concluded that the trackway data "suggests a very high proportion of theropod tracks." We used footprint shape and step length rather than lack of claw impressions as the main criteria. The presence or absence of claw impressions is controlled to some degree by the quality of preservation, and their absence cannot be considered a decisive factor in identifying trackmakers as ornithopods.

Too Many Carnivores?

It would have been simpler to explain the dinosaur community if theropod tracks were as rare as we originally thought. In the original interpretations we inferred a predator to prey ratio of about 1:30, similar to the ratio suggested by skeletal remains in the Morrison Formation. The new interpretations suggest a completely different ratio of about 60:40. What kind of bizarre animal community contains so many predators? There are two possible interpretations that could help explain this anomaly. First, the 60:40 predator to prey ratio is based on counting the number of trackmakers, not the size or "biomass" of the animals. At the Purgatoire Tracksite, the average size of the carnivores (predators) is much less than that of the herbivores (prey). The footprint length of the carnivorous theropods averages about 37 centimeters (about 14 inches), which is about half the average sauropod track length of about 67 centimeters (about 26 inches). However, an animal that is twice as long as another is much more than twice its volume. As a general rule, any single linear dimension such as footprint length can be squared to give a corresponding area (for example footprint area) and cubed to give a corresponding volume of the animal. Thus an animal with a footprint

Dinosaur Biomass

Despite the popular notion that all dinosaurs were large creatures, they ranged from chicken-sized up to super, giant sauropods that weighed as much as 50 tons. A small chicken-sized dinosaur with feet less than 10 centimeters (4 inches) in length probably weighed only about 10 pounds, only about 1/10,000 of the weight of a full-grown 50-ton (100,000 pound) brachiosaur. Even when comparing the larger bipedal dinosaurs from the Purgatoire site (average foot length of 67 centimeters or 26 inches), we find significant differences in weight estimates. According to the studies of Australian dinosaur tracker Tony Thulborn, a 37-centimeter-long (14.5 inch) theropod track would correspond to an animal that stood about 1.8 meters (6 feet) at the hip and weighed about 1 ton. By contrast, a sauropod with a foot length of 67 centimeters, (26 inches) [or two-thirds of the maximum adult length of about 100 centimeters (39 inches)] would, in theory, be about one-third of the maximum body mass. As estimates for the weight of full-grown sauropods range from about 12 to 50 tons, the estimated weight of the average-sized Purgatoire sauropod would be between about 4 and 16 tons. The average of these two extreme estimates is 10 tons or 10 times the average theropod biomass. This gives us a predator to prey ratio of 6:40 instead of 60:40—a result similar to the idealized model just presented.

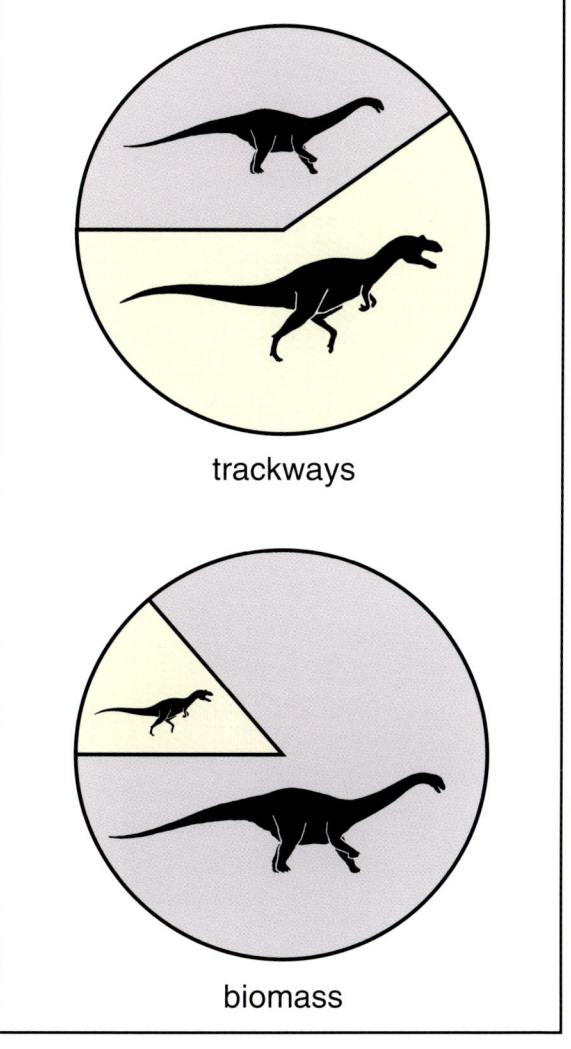

trackways

biomass

length twice that of another might have four times the footprint area and eight times the volume. This would mean that the 60:40 ratio for number of trackways would be adjusted to a 60:40x8 (equal to 60:320 or 1:5.3) biomass ratio of predator to prey, using the simple example of the predator having average foot lengths that were half that of the prey. Clearly a 1:5.3 ratio estimate is fundamentally different from a 6:4 ratio, and is more typical of the biomass estimates derived from counting skeletons.

Until recently few trackers bothered to count trackways systematically, and the calculation of biomass from such counts had never been undertaken. Our interpretation of the Purgatoire dinosaur population based on these counts of trackways is much more consistent with expected predator to prey ratios (see box on page 39).

One other possible explanation for the large number of theropod trackways relative to those made by sauropods, is the hypothesis that theropods were more active. A number of trackers find support for this in the observation that some modern animals are much more active than others. For example, a chipmunk is more active than a buffalo and a small sandpiper is more active than a large heron. Many authorities note that theropods were probably very active animals and were, in most cases, well designed for speed.

Paleontologists have also noted that many theropods had large eyes and were primarily visual hunters, relying less on sound and smell than on sight. Such attributes would have equipped them well for patrolling open areas to locate potential prey. The limey mudflats that surrounded Dinosaur Lake would probably have been an ideal location for theropods to survey the lay of the land. It is therefore not surprising that their tracks are so common at the site.

WHAT ELSE TRACKS TELL US

Dinosaur Social Behavior

The large number of tracks on the shores of Dinosaur Lake indicate that dinosaurs were quite abundant in the area and that there was probably balance between predators and prey. We also know something about the locomotion of individual animals. Theropods were relatively fast moving, very erect bipeds, whereas sauropods were slower quadrupeds. But how did individuals of a particular type interact? Did both theropods and sauropods travel individually or in groups? The social behavior of dinosaurs is an intriguing and popular topic that can be studied seriously using trackway evidence.

The evidence at Dinosaur Lake shows that theropod trackways have little in the way of regular patterns. We find a couple of parallel trackways, but there are not enough tracks preserved to demonstrate an obvious trend, and no indication that they consistently moved in the same direction. This suggests that individuals were crisscrossing the area in a more or less random fashion and it is hard to infer any kind of social behavior.

However, the sauropod trackway evidence presents quite a different picture. There are a significant number of parallel trackways heading toward the west. One group of five trackways has become particularly famous as an example of social behavior. The pattern is interpreted as an example of social behavior because:

- all the trackways are of the same type, size, and depth, and because
- the trackways never cross or deviate from one another—the spacing between them is remarkably regular.

It seems unlikely that five or more animals, all of the same type and size, moving in the exact same direction and making tracks of the same depth, were not moving as a herd or social group. Put another way, could five individuals pass by at different times and leave such a pattern? Each animal would have had to deliberately travel a couple of yards to the right or left of existing trackways, and there is no evidence of dinosaurs or other animals doing this. We conclude, therefore, that these sauropods moved as a group. We can also refer to them as an age group because they were all quite small, with feet about 50 centimeters (20 inches) long—half the length of the largest animals of that type. In some publications they have been referred to as juveniles or sub-adults.

Bronto Buddies

Trackway evidence of gregarious behavior among sauropods is quite common. When Roland Bird published his first report on Cretaceous sauropod tracks from Texas, he reported 12 parallel sauropod trackways. In a subsequent report he recorded 23 parallel trackways at another Texas site. This is how he became famous as the originator of the "herding brontosaur" hypothesis. Some paleontologists have suggested that the Texas sites show the herd structured with large individuals on the periphery protecting younger

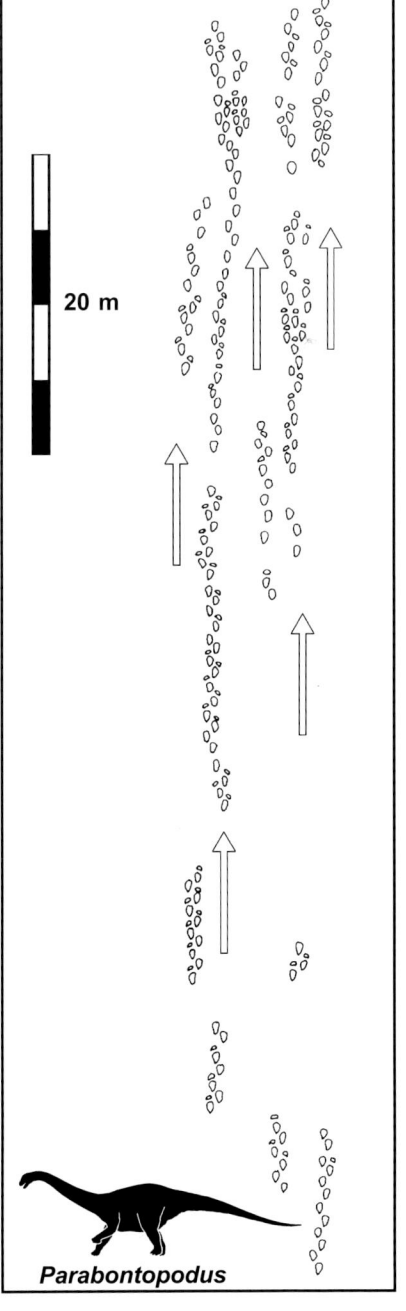

Trackway map of the brontosaur social group. Arrows show the trend of each animal's trackway.

20 m

Parabontopodus

Missed Opportunities: Science in Purgatory

Dinosaur tracker Roland T. Bird with a brontosaur track from the Texas site.

Roland Bird and his boss, Barnum Brown, never recognized the full potential of the Purgatoire site and so never returned to study it and compare it with the Texas sites Bird made so famous. This missed opportunity meant that observations that could have been made in the 1930s were not made until the 1980s. Scientific study of the tracks was postponed for 50 years—waiting in "Purgatory."

In addition to Bird's not clearly recognizing that the Purgatoire tracks were the first brontosaur tracks ever recorded, and that they indicated social behavior, an even more bizarre chain of events unfolded as the Texas study progressed. With the substantial backing of the American Museum of Natural History in New York, Bird was able to excavate a segment of brontosaur trackway along with a parallel segment of a theropod trackway and ship it to New York for display. There it was to be exhibited with sauropod and theropod skeletons mounted in the tracks. The problem was that no Cretaceous skeletons were known from Texas or from rocks of this age anywhere in the world. So the museum had to get Jurassic "Brontosaurus" and *Allosaurus* skeletons from the Morrison Formation instead. This makes for a very incongruous exhibit—rather like mounting the skeleton of our 3-million-year-old ancestor Lucy in the footprints of moon-walking astronauts! A giant step forward in time for a brontosaur, but a very small step for science. Had Bird been able to study and excavate or replicate tracks from the Purgatoire site, he could have mounted these skeletons in footprints of the right age.

Perhaps these thoughts were also on Bird's mind. Long after his Texas study, in his autobiography, published posthumously in 1985, he wrote that from time to time "My thoughts flashed back to the round tracks on the Purgatory River."

ones in the center. A careful study of the tracks and maps does not support this interesting speculation.

Despite the fact that the Cretaceous trackway evidence from Texas is famous, no reports of parallel sauropod trackways from the Jurassic were published until the Purgatoire Tracksite was restudied. It is interesting to note this fact, because Bird visited the Purgatoire Tracksite before he went to Texas. Had he looked a little more closely, he might have reported Jurassic sauropod social behavior fifty years before it was recognized. The simple conclusion is that some sauropods were already gregarious by Jurassic times and continued to be so during the Cretaceous. In recent years other examples of parallel sauropod trackways have been reported from Jurassic sites in Europe.

Brontosaurs traveling together as a social group. Artwork by Douglas Henderson.

Dinosaur Speed

In 1976, the British zoologist R. McNeill Alexander proposed a formula for calculating the speed of animals from their trackways. He applied this formula to a few dinosaur trackways and developed the first estimates of dinosaur speed. Since then, many people have used his formula, though other similar formulae have also been proposed, and many speed estimates for dinosaurs have been published.

To calculate the speed of a dinosaur using a trackway, measure footprint length and stride (two steps), and using a pocket calculator, multiply the footprint length by four to get an estimate of the hip height. Apply these measurements to the following formula:

$$v = 0.25 \; g^{0.5} \; x \; sl^{1.67} \; x \; h^{-1.17}$$

where v=velocity (or speed), g=the acceleration due to gravity (9.8 m/sec²), sl=stride length, and h=estimated hip height (or four times footprint length). The final result is in meters per second. Multiplying that figure by 3.6 gives kilometers per hour. For example, a brontosaur with a foot length of about 75 centimeters and a stride of 250 centimeters has an estimated speed of about 1.0 meters per second or 3.6 kilometers per hour (about 2.2 miles per hour). Remember that the final result is only an estimate and that other formulae may produce slightly different results.

The stride length of a walking theropod is shorter than the stride length of a running one.

The results of estimating speed from many dinosaur trackways show that most dinosaurs were walking most of the time. This doesn't mean

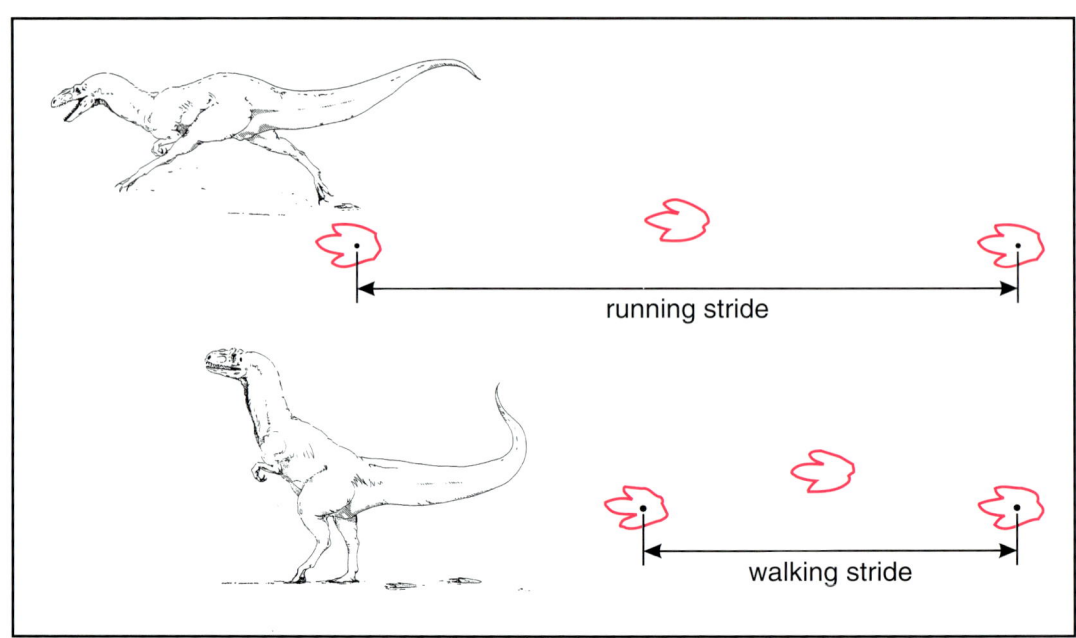

running stride

walking stride

they could not run but only that they didn't run very often. In fact, the only good trackway evidence for running dinosaurs comes from a theropod trackway in Texas where the trackmaker was doing an estimated 40 kilometers per hour or about 25 miles per hour—about the speed of an Olympic sprinter running 100 meters (110 yards) in 10 seconds. All known trackways of sauropods and other quadrupedal dinosaurs indicate that the animals were walking.

Estimates of speed from Purgatoire theropod trackways fall in the range of 6 to 10 kilometers per hour (about 4 to 6 miles per hour), indicating a brisk walk, but not a run. Estimates for the brontosaurs are somewhat slower—ranging from 3 to 6 kilometers per hour (2 to 4 miles per hour). No one has ever found brontosaur trackways that provided estimates much beyond this speed.

Other Evidence of Dinosaurs

It is common to find at least one feature that is difficult to interpret at most paleontological sites. The Purgatoire Tracksite is no exception, for it reveals a very odd bathtub-sized structure that defies an obvious explanation. The depression is about 3 meters long by 1.5 meters wide (10 feet by 5 feet) and about 1 foot deep in the center, with sides that slope at 20 to 25 degrees all round. At first sight this structure appears about the right size and shape to be a depression where a dinosaur had lain down. However, such features are virtually unknown. Moreover, the impression, seen on top of track bed 2, is too deep to have been made by an animal lying down. If a large animal chose to lie down in very soft mud it could conceivably leave such an impression, but not on firm sand-textured sediment such as that in bed 2. Besides, the indentation is filled with the same sediment as the layer in which it is made.

A dinosaur-sized depression in the rock poses a problem for interpretation.

One conceivable explanation is that a dead animal lay in the shallows near the lake shore as the sand-grade sediment was washed in to a depth of about one foot all around it. This could happen around a live animal that was lying in the shallows or around a grounded carcass that had floated into shallow water. In either case, the carcass (or animal) would then have had to float away again (or somehow be removed) in order for more of the same sediment to wash in and fill the depression.

This scenario is purely speculative, and we don't imply that it is probable. In fact, there are virtually no convincing reports of dinosaur body impressions made by animals lying down, because if they did lie down on firm ground, they must have spread their weight too much to leave deep or clear impressions. On the other hand, the depression just described is the right size to fit the body of a large dinosaur, at a site where abundant traces of dinosaurs are found. In the final analysis, we do not know what caused this feature to form.

Trampling

Anyone can recognize a dinosaur trackway when it is clearly impressed on a flat surface. However, experience has taught us that many surfaces are irregular and that trackers must look hard to find clear footprint evidence. As more and more dinosaur tracksites have been discovered,

trackers have had more opportunity to recognize tracks that are not so obvious and well preserved. Trackers have also learned to recognize layers that have been trampled, churned up, or stomped by the activity of numerous animals. Such trampling can be difficult to study scientifically, but it is nevertheless interesting from several viewpoints.

The difficulty involved in the study of trampling is that large animals make a mess of flat layers of strata, making them hard to interpret. How do you count

Trampling of the surface on some layers at Purgatoire is nearly 100 percent.

tracks or measure such a disorganized mess? The first step is trying to assess how much sediment was disturbed. Geologists refer to the disturbance of sediments by plant roots, burrowing animals, and trackmakers as "bioturbation." The disturbance caused by large vertebrates has been called plowing, churning, stomping, or trampling, or in more technical terms, "mega-bioturbation." A similar term, "dinoturbation," has been used when the trackmakers were obviously dinosaurs. Dinoturbation can be measured by the percentage of a surface covered by tracks. At the Purgatoire site, both lowermost and uppermost track layers were so heavily trampled that 100 percent of the surface was disturbed.

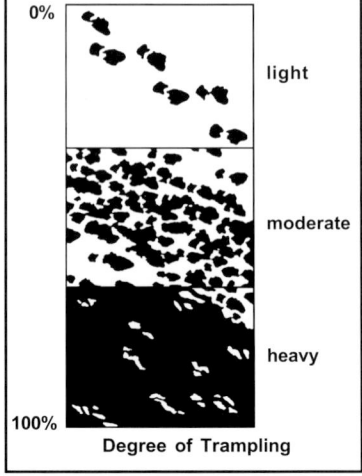

0%

light

moderate

heavy

100%

Degree of Trampling

Despite the extensive trampling, it has been possible to find segments of both sauropod and theropod trackways in the lowest level. The small tracks of theropods or other bipedal dinosaurs are interesting because they are so rare in other layers at the Purgatoire Tracksite. They probably owe their preservation to a softer, more yielding substrate. In addition, these different sediments probably represent a slightly different lake shore environment from that represented by the other layers. We think these differences are important.

Dinosaurs not only trampled sediments, they also trampled plants and animals such as snails, clams, frogs, and even turtles and crocodiles. At the Purgatoire Tracksite there is evidence of both plants of the "horsetail" variety and clams having been trampled in bed 1. In fact, the Purgatoire Tracksite provided one of the first fossil examples of trampled clams ever reported. In one area of bed 1, more than two dozen clams, related to the modern genus *Unio*, were trampled and killed by sauropods. Modern unionid clams live in freshwater rivers and lakes and have a distinctive orientation or "life position" in the sediment, with their front end down and their rear end sticking up into the water. None of the clams in this area are found in life position. They have all been crushed or pushed aside by brontosaur foot falls. All have both of their shells together and no sediment inside. This is good evidence that they were killed quickly and buried on the spot. Clams that die naturally often open up, and their shells separate from one another as the flesh and ligaments decay. Modern studies show that these same types of clams often get trampled by horses and cows at river crossings. Sometimes they survive despite broken shells that heal in irregular shapes. Such wounded survivors have been described as "Molluscan Monstrosities." Those from the Purgatoire Tracksite

The small tracks of theropods or other bipedal dinosaurs are found along with sauropod tracks in the lowest track layer at Purgatoire. These tracks are rare in other layers.

Evidence of clams that were trampled and killed by sauropods have been found at the tracksite.

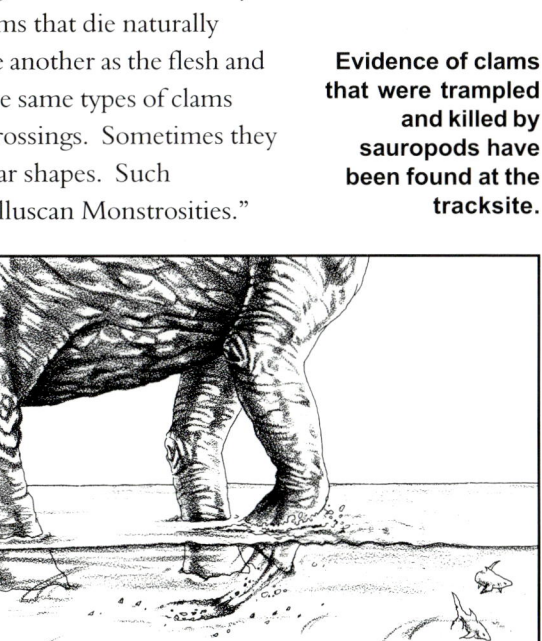

evidently did not heal and could perhaps be called "Molluscan Mortalities."

There are also many plant stem and root impressions associated with trampled bed 1. Obviously it would be impossible for large brontosaurs to walk along vegetated lake shores without trampling plants. Some authors have even suggested that dinosaur trampling stimulated plant growth, rather like pruning, and that only those plants that could regenerate quickly were successful over time.

Bones to Fit the Tracks

Paleontologists generally believe that bones and footprints are not found together. While this is often true, there are notable exceptions, such as the Purgatoire site. In the mid-1980s, bones were found in the tracksite area during the final phase of footprint mapping. They were recovered from bed 4, and subsequent study shows that they are the remains of the left hind limb of a sauropod. These remains include most of the foot, and parts of the long bones of the leg.

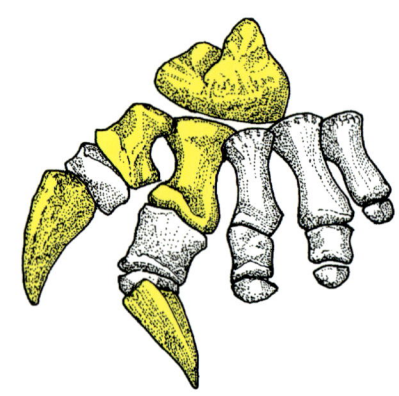

Preserved bones noted in color.

Bed 4 shows unmistakable signs of heavy trampling. As a result, these bones have been broken and disturbed. Trampling also makes it harder to remove the bones from the rock, because they are fragmented and broken, rather than whole.

The foot remains found at Purgatoire consist of at least ten bones including various ankle bones and the large claws found on a sauropod hind foot. The species of dinosaur represented by the foot bones is not currently known. Sauropod foot bones are not as well-known as other parts of the skeleton, and there is a lack of detailed study by specialists. Another problem with identifying sauropods from hind feet,

One of the claws found.

is that many of the elements are very similar, even in different families. Finding more parts of the foot, and further study of what we have already found, may eventually lead to identifying the specific animal.

It is intriguing to think that we might soon connect a foot to the many tracks found nearby. However, if we do identify the species, it does not automatically mean that we can link the bones to the footprints. Probably several species of sauropod visited Dinosaur Lake, most leaving their footprints, but at least one dying near the shore and leaving its bones for posterity.

The End of the Trail

There is abundant track evidence at the Purgatoire Tracksite that provides much food for thought for professional paleontologists, teachers, dinosaur enthusiasts, and visitors. As this guide has shown, the track evidence is quite complex and sometimes ambiguous. Moreover, it involves a combination of geological and biological evidence. For these reasons we must be careful not to read too much into the interpretation of particular trackways at the site.

Tracks were made by living animals and obviously represent behavior. It is therefore tempting to interpret dinosaur tracks in terms of dynamic and exciting activity. The Purgatoire Tracksite provides some examples, such as the group of young sauropods moving west as a herd. However, so far, there is no sensational or dramatic evidence of predators attacking prey, high-speed chases, or mothers rounding up babies. We would love to find such track evidence, but it has not been found at the Purgatoire site—or any other sites.

Instead, we can weave together a complex, and perhaps richer, picture of life at Dinosaur Lake. Against the backdrop of a Jurassic lake environment inhabited by various plants, molluscs, arthropods, fish, and dinosaurs, we can build a picture of continuous and subtle changes in the configuration of the lake shore for a time span equivalent to several—probably many—dinosaur generations. Sometimes we get clear glimpses of short episodes of dinosaur activity. These snapshots of life at Dinosaur Lake splice together into a series of frames. Not quite a complete movie, but nevertheless real scenes from the rich tapestry of life that surrounded Dinosaur Lake. Our story goes like this:

Episode 1: The Dinosaurs' First Visit to Dinosaur Lake.

At this time the lake was becoming more shallow and a fine limey mud was accumulating in the lake. After a long period of relatively high water, clams were established residents near a vegetated shoreline that sprouted small horsetails about as big around as your finger and probably 1.5 meters (4 or 5 feet) tall. The limey mud in the shallows was soft and sticky, but the water was clear and fresh. There was also plenty of oxygen in the water, allowing fish, clams, snails, and crustaceans to thrive.

The lake was inviting to dinosaurs and other vertebrates, for almost certainly they could drink the water. Tracks are found in abundance in these limey sediments and are a sure sign of potable water—in Africa today the abundance and variety of tracks around lakes is a measure of the water quality. Amongst the horsetails and other plants, turkey- and emu-sized theropods left a variety of tracks that even in Jurassic times may have been indistinct and muddled. The smaller animals may have been completely hidden in the vegetation. No doubt the carnivores took advantage of any food sources available, including fish, insects, and trampled clams. Evidence from other sites suggest that frogs and other small vertebrates were common in lake and pond environments.

Brontosaurs were the most abundant herbivores, and their numerous tracks show that they trampled through this limey mud, both in the shallows where the sediment was softer and on the firmer footing above the waterline. They passed by in groups and individually and extensively trampled the vegetation.

Episode 2: Dinosaur Visits Two through Four.

For a few years the shoreline scene shifted away from the place where the Purgatoire flows past Rock Crossing. Water level rose and expanded the lake towards the south. After awhile the lake level dropped again and the shoreline edged back to the area of Rock Crossing. A little muddy limestone accumulated in the shallows not far from the shore, and large dinosaurs waded in, leaving very deep footprints (Visit Two).

Soon conditions changed again along the lakeshore, and a new type of limey sediment began to accumulate. It was coarse-textured, like sand, and contained bits of clam and snail shell as well as gravel-sized lumps of algae composed of pure limestone. Also mixed in were ooids, sure signs of a shallow lake where the limey sand was moved around regularly by waves. Ripple marks also provide evidence that the waters were agitated by waves and currents.

As the sand was washed back and forth, it produced even, flat surfaces on which dinosaurs walked both during and after the final accumulation of the layer (Visits Three and Four). Over much of the area the surface was quite firm—too firm to allow small dinosaurs to produce clear tracks—but to the north the tracks get deeper, indicating a wetter substrate. The majority of brontosaurs that crossed the area appear to have been moving west, and on at least one occasion a group of five or more juveniles moved west, leaving perfectly parallel trackways.

All the brontosaurs left narrow-gauge trackways, perhaps indicating that they were all of the same type, although they varied considerably in size. In addition to at least forty of these individuals, about sixty theropods also crossed the area moving in all different directions. In a relatively short period of time, at least a hundred animals crossed a stretch of shoreline of less than one-half kilometer (one-quarter mile) long. No doubt the wave-agitated waters were still suitable to drink despite lower lake levels.

Episode 3: Dinosaur Visits Five and Six.

The lake level rose and dropped again—first bringing mud into the area, and then more sandy-textured limestone. This time the sediment contained lots of fish scales, probably indicating that a lot of fish had recently died in the lake, perhaps during the most recent drop in water level or as the result of some other environmental stress. Plants encroached on the lakeshore, sending out horizontal roots—a sign that the water table was still high. A few dinosaurs left indistinct tracks on the firm sediment.

Conditions changed again, but this time more subtly, producing more sandy limestone and an accumulation of fine limey mud rather than shale. This indicates that lake levels did not rise much. At least two dinosaurs (one a brontosaur) came into the area and died. The brontosaur was not ripped apart and scattered by predators or scavengers—at least not to any great degree—for we find most of the hind limb intact. However, many brontosaurs came into the area and trampled these sediments, damaging and disturbing the bones where they lay and obliterating most of the ripple marks and other evidence of the sedimentary history of the layers.

Thus, the track story of Dinosaur Lake ends as it began, with abundant evidence of dinosaur activity along the shores of a living lake.

OTHER DINOSAUR TRACKS IN THE AREA

The Purgatoire Tracksite represents the middle of the "Age of Dinosaurs" (the Mesozoic Era) or the Jurassic Period. However, fossil footprints from the Triassic Period and Cretaceous Period are also known in this general area of southeastern Colorado.

Tracks known as *Grallator*; made by a chicken-sized carnivorous dinosaur.

The oldest tracks represent the very end of the Triassic Period (or Late Triassic Epoch, about 220- to 208-million years ago). The richest area for tracks is one bounded by Kenton, Oklahoma, Prichett, Colorado, and Folsom, New Mexico. The best-known, and best preserved tracks are of the type known as *Grallator*. The name refers to their resemblance to tracks made by the family of birds known as the Grallidae, which includes various waders and waterbirds. The tracks differ from those of modern waterbirds in not having such widely splayed digits. Tracks of this type were among the first ever discovered in North America—in the early 1800s—and are now known to represent small carnivorous dinosaurs about the size of chickens. Other dinosaur tracks from this tri-state area represent larger carnivorous dinosaurs the size of emus. They are all found in rocks of the Chinle Group, which are famous for containing the fossil logs of the Petrified Forest in northeastern Arizona.

Unfortunately, none of the sites with *Grallator* tracks are on public land and accessible to visitors. They are, however, an integral part of the track record of the southeastern high plains, and show that various ancestral species of carnivorous dinosaur had a long history, extending back as much as 60- to 70-million years before they made tracks at the Purgatoire Tracksite.

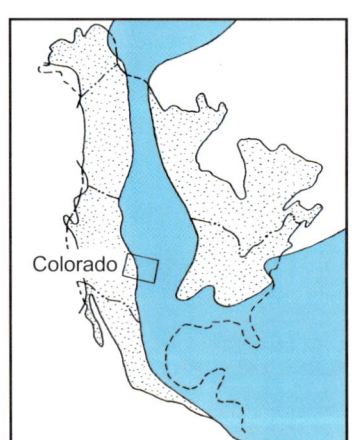

The Cretaceous Western Interior Seaway.

Tracks from the end of the Age of Dinosaurs represent two epochs: the Early Cretaceous and the Late Cretaceous. In southeastern Colorado, Early Cretaceous footprints (about 100-million years old) occur mainly in strata known as the Dakota Group. Tracks in this unit of rock form part of an extensive carpet of tracks known as the "Dinosaur Freeway." These layers have nothing to do with the Purgatoire Tracksite, which represents a much older (150-million years) lake shore. Instead, the Dinosaur Freeway represents a marine coastline or coastal plain formed when a seaway encroached into the interior of western North America. Referred to as the Cretaceous Western Interior Seaway, it represents the Cretaceous equivalent of the Gulf of Mexico.

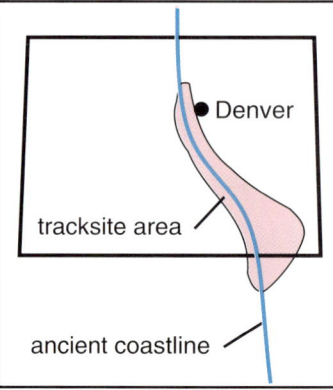

Tracksites show a possible dinosaur migration route along the shoreline of the Cretaceous inland sea.

The most common tracks on the Dinosaur Freeway are those of an Early Cretaceous duck-billed dinosaur that probably resembled the herbivore *Iguanodon*. Parallel trackways show that these animals were gregarious, like brontosaurs. Other trackmakers at this time include ostrich-like carnivorous dinosaurs, crocodiles, and rare waterbirds. The Dinosaur Freeway extends all the way from the Denver area to the tri-state area around Clayton, New Mexico. Sites accessible to the public can be found at Dinosaur Ridge near Denver and at Clayton Lake State Park in New Mexico.

Tracks from the final, Late Cretaceous Epoch of the Age of Dinosaurs can be found in coal-rich strata known as the Raton Formation in the region of Raton, New Mexico, and Trinidad, Colorado. This formation contains the famous Cretaceous-Tertiary (or K-T) boundary marking the extinction of the dinosaurs. Recent work has shown that dinosaur tracks are common just below this boundary layer, proving that dinosaurs were abundant until the very end of the epoch. The most common tracks appear to be those of hadrosaurs, another type of duck-billed dinosaur descended from the Early Cretaceous iguanodontids. Tracks of horned dinosaurs, possibly *Triceratops*, are also found, and the first convincing example of a *Tyrannosaurus rex* track was reported in 1993 near Cimarron, southwest of Raton.

Iguanodon-like creatures may have migrated along the shoreline of the inland sea. Artwork by John Sibbick.

Martin Lockley with a replica of the first *Tyrannosaurus rex* track to be found.

The Concerns

Conservation versus Public
Education and Enjoyment

PROBLEMS OF EROSION

Since the Purgatoire Valley Dinosaur Tracksite was rediscovered in 1982, it has presented an interesting conservation dilemma. The site is situated in a river bed, with horizontal layers of alternating limestone and shale. Most of the dinosaur tracks are found in limestone bed 2, which is incised by the Purgatoire River and can be seen on both banks. The tracks are subject to continuous erosion and weathering, and a major portion of the trackway has been destroyed over the past 50 years due to erosive river flow and annual flooding. Erosion originally uncovered the site, but it is now also steadily destroying it. Normal erosion can cut back exposed ledges of strata by several feet in a decade, while periodic heavy flooding can accomplish the same devastating results in a few hours. During high-velocity flood flows, the soft, highly erodible shales are easily removed, and the track-bearing limestone beds above are undercut. As a result, the limestones fracture along intersecting vertical joints and large blocks of limestone fall into the river and are swept downstream, destroying a valuable paleontological resource.

The soft shale layers are eroded away by river flow and flooding, undercutting the limestone track beds.

Wear, caused by visitor's use, also contributes to the degradation of the tracksite. The U.S. Forest Service presently offers guided vehicle

tours to the tracksite, and the area is accessible by bicycle, horseback, or hiking. Visitors are allowed to walk on and explore the trackways without restriction, and there are no well-defined trails. Unescorted visitors should make every effort to avoid causing further track erosion. One way for the visitor to help the conservation effort is to avoid walking on the edges of track-bearing layers on the river bank. Avoid cleaning out tracks too

vigorously to observe or photograph them. This accelerates the loosening and separation of bits of the surface. Be patient and wait for good low-angle light on tracks that are naturally exposed.

Natural erosive agents also contribute to tracksite erosion. These include plants that grow in the limestone beds and normal weathering agents such as freezing and thawing of the rock, wind, and water. The non-native tamarisk plant is probably the greatest biological risk because it grows between the limestone blocks on the tracksite. In addition, cattle sometimes slip through fences that have not been maintained, and graze in the area around the tracksite. Livestock trampling presents a danger to track conservation, and efforts are underway to address this problem.

Scientists, conservationists, and land management agencies are therefore faced with the dilemma of how to preserve this valuable fossil resource. The scientific solution and first step is the easiest and cheapest preservation method. It involves obtaining information and compiling as much documentation as possible. This field guide is an example. The Forest Service encourages continuing research at the tracksite and at other paleontological resource locations as they become known. A Memorandum of Understanding exists between the Forest Service and other agencies to promote management of fossils on public lands and encourage documentation and coordination with academia, professional societies, and industry. The second step—how to stop or slow erosion—is more difficult. River erosion cannot be completely stopped unless the stream is diverted. A third option—to make a replica or remove the entire rock layer—would be extremely expensive and impractical. The last option to preserve the tracks would be to bury them, which defeats the objective of public education at the site.

The undercutting of the limestone beds causes blocks containing trackways to break off and fall into the river.

PICKET WIRE CANYONLANDS MANAGEMENT PLAN

In 1990, Congress passed Public Law 101-510, which transferred approximately 16,700 acres of the Pinon Canyon Maneuver Site from the Army to the Comanche National Grasslands to be managed by the U.S. Forest Service. The land parcels transferred are referred to as the Picket Wire Canyonlands. This legislation required development of a management plan for those parcels of land in the Purgatoire River Canyon where there are significant and unique paleontological, heritage (cultural), and natural

resources. The legislation also states that the plan must include a survey and inventory of the area's paleontological and archaeological resources, and a strategy for protecting and conserving the dinosaur tracksite in the Purgatoire River Valley along with other paleontological and archaeological resources in the Picket Wire Canyonlands.

The Comanche National Grassland Picket Wire Canyonlands Management Plan was completed in 1994. The U.S. Forest Service considers this plan to be an interim strategy until the Forest Plan is revised—tentatively toward the end of the decade. The Management Plan outlines the following goals:

- Conserve and protect paleontological resources,
- Conserve and protect heritage (archaeological and historical) resources,
- Maintain ecosystem health,
- Maintain visual quality,
- Provide recreation opportunities,
- Seek public participation through volunteers and partnerships,
- Achieve optimum land ownership and access, and
- Encourage research, educational, and interpretive opportunities.

The plan discusses in detail the existing and desired conditions for each goal, as well as management options and proposed actions, with some estimated costs. Specific actions to protect the site have been proposed, such as the removal and control of the vegetation that is weakening the limestone layers, redirecting the stream flow energy away from the eroding edge of the tracksite, prohibiting the collection or casting of specimens without authorization, and educating the public on the significance of the tracksite. Another important strategy is to implement research efforts that will insure that a complete scientific record of the site is available—one that is sufficient to reconstruct the tracksite and its context. This record includes aerial photographs and maps, close-range maps of footprints in contour, the cataloguing of specimens and molds collected, and the recovery of track-bearing limestone blocks from the riverbed. The proposed actions also consider the other paleontological remains and cultural resources.

Aerial photo of the tracksite area; courtesy of the U.S. Forest Service Geometronics Group.

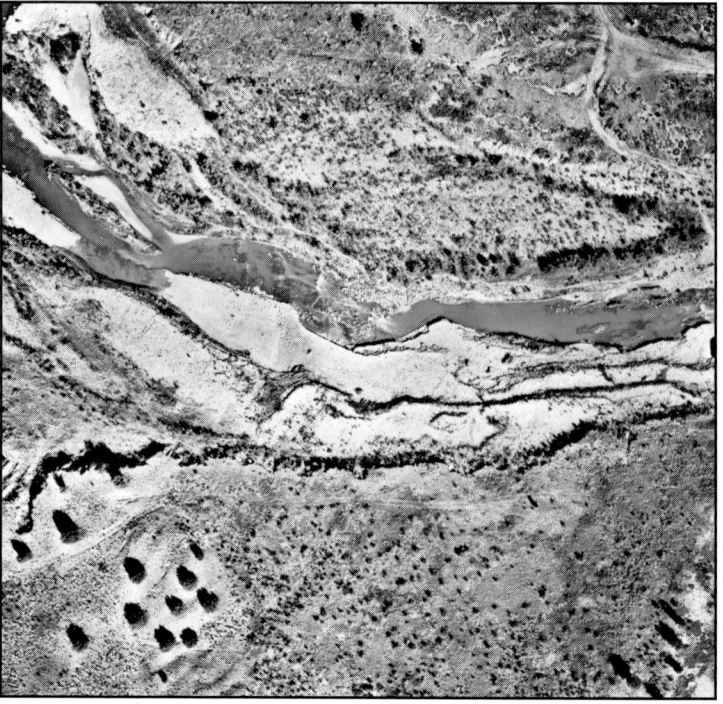

One example of how technology is being applied to record specific data at the site is in the contour mapping of individual footprints using photogrammetry. Stereo photos are taken of significant individual tracks with a special camera whose focal length and other lens characteristics are precisely calibrated. These photos are then observed in an instrument that can make accurate three-dimensional measurements of the photographed objects and store the data electronically. This data can be used for analysis and reconstruction of the track, and is easier to store than actual casts.

The photogrammetry process from photo (left) to contour map of a theropod track (below); courtesy of the U.S. Forest Service Geometronics Group.

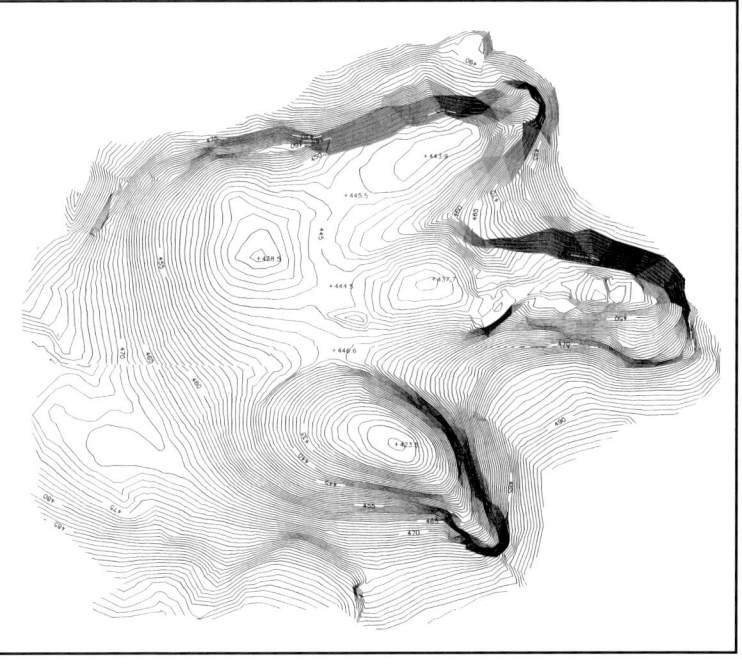

In order to protect and conserve precious, non-renewable resources in the canyon, certain activities are prohibited, and other activities are permitted only if certain conditions are met. Only authorized motorized vehicles are allowed in the Picket Wire Canyonlands. This authorization may be permitted for scholarly research, public education, and recreation as long as it does not interfere with the Army's use of the Pinon Canyon Maneuver Site, across which is the only access for motorized vehicles. Furthermore, vehicle access cannot be allowed to impair the conservation and protection of paleontological, archaeological, or natural resources of the area. Public access to the Picket Wire is discussed more specifically in the next section.

A dusk to dawn closure is in effect for the Picket Wire, both under the Comanche and Cimarron National Grasslands, Pike and San Isabel National Forests Closure Order number 91-10. Vandalism, defacement, or theft are concerns and should be reported to the U.S. Forest Service Office in La Junta, (719) 384-2181, or Springfield, (719) 523-6591.

PUBLIC ACCESS
AND OTHER
UNRESOLVED ISSUES

The Purgatoire Tracksite is in an isolated area, 23 miles from La Junta. Access is both limited and physically difficult. There are two routes into the area, one through Iron Canyon and another through Withers Canyon. Access by these routes is limited by the terrain, Forest Service closures, and Army administrative polices. The Iron Canyon route crosses the Army's Pinon Canyon Maneuver Site and access is through locked gates by permission only. Because the Army has absolute priority in using the Pinon Canyon Maneuver Site, guided auto tours are difficult because they must be booked months in advance and may be cancelled at the last moment if the Army schedules a maneuver. In addition, this tour requires a four-wheel-drive vehicle and a Forest Service guide, also subject to availability.

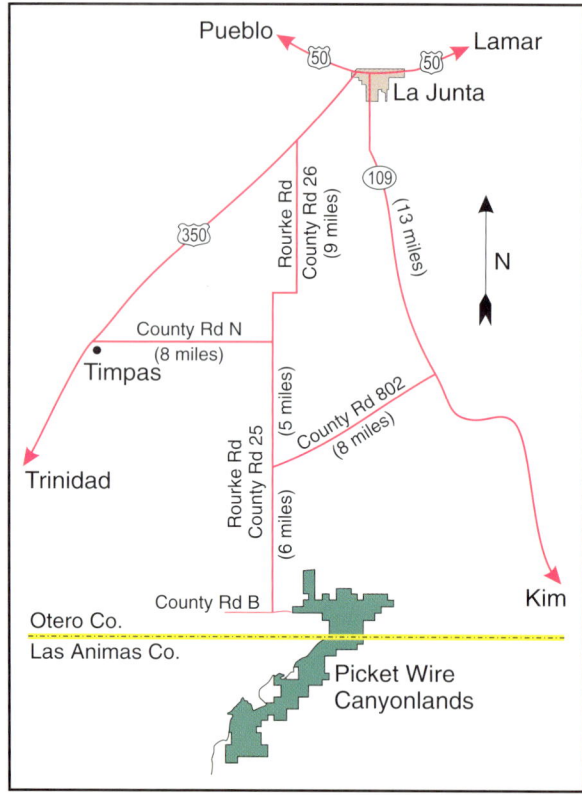

Road directions to the Picket Wire Canyonlands.

To overcome this limitation and accommodate the public's desire to view the dinosaur tracksite, rock art, and other heritage resources, the Forest Service has established a second access to the area through Withers Canyon that is open daily. Withers Canyon is the only allowable access to the Canyonlands for the general public, and access is allowed only by foot, mountain bike, or horseback at the present time. This access is quite lengthy—10.6 miles roundtrip from the head of Withers Canyon to the tracksite. The length of the hike can increase to 16.6 miles roundtrip from the bulletin board to the tracksite, depending on the road conditions from Withers to the bulletin board. Although the trail follows a dirt road it is rough in places, changes in elevation about 500 feet, is not well marked, and can be hazardous in a thunderstorm when the roads and trails become muddy and flashfloods occur. During the summer, heat, lack of drinkable water, and the presence of rattlesnakes make this hike hazardous. This access is not suitable for school groups, the disabled, or anyone in poor physical condition.

The current access situation precludes many people from visiting the dinosaur tracksite. Buses and low-clearance vehicles cannot safely negotiate the roads; there are no facilities or trails for the physically challenged; and reservations for guided auto tours must be booked months in advance. The long hike prevents many visitors, particularly children and the elderly, from enjoying the tracksite.

There are several other conflicts and issues in the management of the tracksite. Private landowners are concerned about trespassing on private property, littering, and the potential for accidental wildland fires. Conservation groups are concerned about visitor impact on the natural resources. The Army cannot allow public access to affect its training missions.

It is important to remember to have as little an impact as possible while visiting the paleontological, archaeological, and historical sites of the area. We want you to enjoy these wonderful resources—as much and as often as you like—but we would also like your children and grandchildren to enjoy them just as much. If you are able to visit the tracksite, please do not take anything other than photos, and do not make casts of the dinosaur tracks, or rubbings or otherwise touch the rock art or other artifacts you may see.

Hike With Care

Take Only Photos

Don't Touch

Access routes into the Picket Wire.

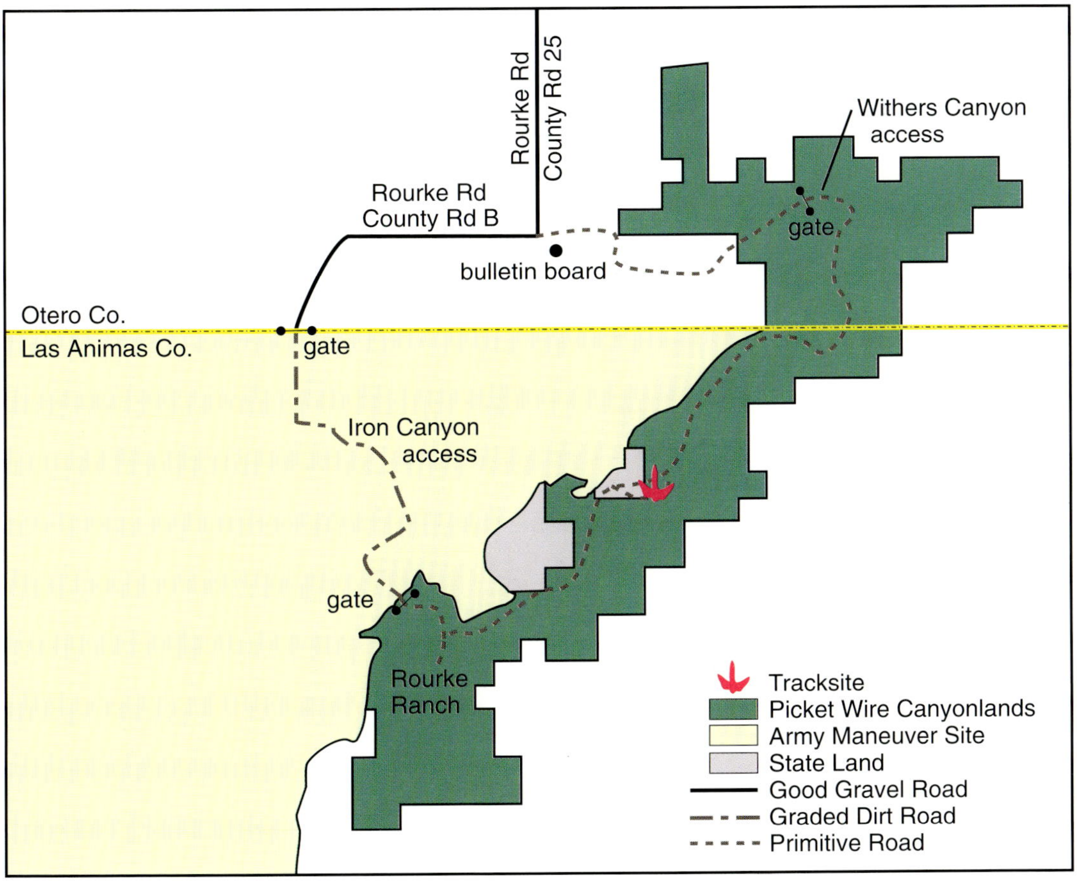

Rourke Rd
County Rd 25

Withers Canyon
access

Rourke Rd
County Rd B

gate

bulletin board

Otero Co.
Las Animas Co.

gate

Iron Canyon
access

gate

Rourke
Ranch

Tracksite
Picket Wire Canyonlands
Army Maneuver Site
State Land
Good Gravel Road
Graded Dirt Road
Primitive Road

Useful References

There are many references to the Purgatoire Tracksite. Some comprise articles and reports that include a few illustrations and short summaries of features seen at the site. There are also many technical articles on the geology of southeastern Colorado. We have included only those articles and books which provide the most pertinent background information on the site, and the geology, paleontology, and archaeology of the area. Additional references can be found in these articles.

Geologic References

Lee, W. T., 1901, The Morrison Formation of southeastern Colorado: Journal of Geology 9: 343-353. (one of the first reports of Morrison strata in the region)

Lucas, S. G., 1992, Stratigraphy and age of the Triassic Jelm Formation, Wyoming-Colorado: Geological Society of America Abstracts with Program 24(6): 49. (new interpretations of Triassic strata in this region)

Oriel, S. S. and Mudge, M. R., 1956, Problems of lower Mesozoic stratigraphy in southeastern Colorado: Rocky Mountain Association of Geologists Guidebook, p. 19-24. (a paper indicating some of the problems involved in recognizing and interpreting rock formations in the area)

Prince, N. K., 1988, Lacustrine deposition in the Jurassic Morrison Formation, Purgatoire River region, southeastern Colorado: M.S. Thesis, University of Colorado at Denver, 182 p. (a detailed study of the Morrison Formation in the tracksite region)

Scott, G. R., 1968, Geologic and structure contour map of the La Junta Quadrangle, Colorado and Kansas, U.S. Geological Survey Miscellaneous Geological Investigations Map I-560. (the standard geologic map for the area)

Paleontological References

Dodson, P., Behrensmeyer, A. K., Bakker, R. T. and McIntosh, J. S., 1980, Taphonomy and paleoecology of the dinosaur beds of the Jurassic Morrison Formation: Paleobiology, 6: 208-232. (an important study of the relationship between ancient environments and dinosaur types in the Morrison Formation)

Kauffman, E. G. et al., 1986, Geological and paleontological site analysis of the Pinon Canyon Maneuver Site, Las Animas County, Colorado: Unpublished report to the U.S. Army, 132 p. (detailed results of a paleontological survey of the area commissioned by the U.S. Army when they took over management of the area in the 1980s)

Kauffman, E. G., 1977, Geological and biological overview: Western Interior Cretaceous basin: The Mountain Geologist, 14: 75-99. (a useful introduction to the Western Interior Cretaceous Seaway)

Kauffman, E. G., 1977, Illustrated guide to biostratigraphically important Cretaceous macrofossils, Western Interior Basin, USA: The Mountain Geologist, 14: 255-274. (a useful guide to Cretaceous fossils of the area)

Simpson, G. G., The age of the Morrison Formation: American Journal of Science, 21: 198-216. (a classic study showing that dinosaurs from the Morrison are similar to certain forms found in Africa)

Yen, T. C., 1952, Molluscan fauna of the Morrison Formation: U.S. Geological Survey Professional Paper 233B: 21-51. (one of the few papers providing information on clams and snails such as those found at the Purgatoire site)

Trackway References

Bird, R. T., 1985, Bones for Barnum Brown: Texas Christian University Press, 225 p. (Bird relates his visit to the site)

Farlow, J. O. and Lockley, M. G., 1989, Roland T. Bird, Dinosaur Tracker: an appreciation: p. 33-36, in Gillette, D. D. and Lockley, M. G. (eds.) Dinosaur Tracks and Traces: Cambridge University Press, 454 p. (contains the history of Bird's visit to the site)

Gillette, D. D. and Lockley, M. G., (eds.), 1989, Dinosaur tracks and traces: Cambridge, Cambridge University Press, 454 p. (the first modern book on dinosaur tracks—contains references to the Purgatoire site)

Gore, R., 1993, Dinosaurs: National Geographic Magazine, 183(1): 2-53. (references the Purgatoire site)

Lockley, M. G., 1991, Tracking Dinosaurs: Cambridge, Cambridge University Press, 238 p. (the first popular science book on dinosaur tracks)

Lockley, M. G., 1987, Dinosaur Trackways, *in* Czerkas, S. J. and Olsen, E. C. (eds.) Dinosaur Past and Present: Los Angeles County Museum Symposium, p. 80-95. (contains artistic reconstruction of dinosaurs making trails on the shores of Dinosaur Lake)

Lockley, M. G., Farlow, J. O. and Meyer, C., 1994, *Brontopodus* and *Parabrontopodus* Ichnogen nov. and the Significance of Wide and Narrow Gauge Sauropod Trackways, Gaia: Revista de Geociencias, Museu Nacional de Historia Natural, Lisbon, Portugal, 10: 126-134. (the original paper in which narrow-gauge tracks from the Purgatoire site were named *Parabrontopodus*)

Lockley, M. G., Holbrook, J., Hunt, A., Matsukawa, M. and Meyer, C., 1992, The dinosaur freeway: a preliminary report on the Cretaceous Megatracksite, Dakota Group, Rocky Mountain Front Range and Highplains, Colorado, Oklahoma and New Mexico, *in* Flores, R. (ed.) Mesozoic of the Western Interior, p. 39-54. (reports on the widespread distribution of Cretaceous dinosaur tracks throughout the area)

Lockley, M. G., Houck, K. and Prince, N. K., 1986, North America's largest dinosaur tracksite: implications for Morrison Formation Paleo-ecology: Geological Society of America Bulletin 97(10): 1163-1176. (the first scientific report and map of the tracksite)

Lockley, M. G. and Prince, N. K., 1988, The Purgatoire Valley Dinosaur Tracksite Region: Geological Society of America Fieldguide for Centennial Meeting, Denver. Colorado School of Mines Professional Contributions #12, p. 275-287. (the first guide for geologists to the Purgatoire site)

MacClary, J. S., 1938, Dinosaur trails of Purgatory: Scientific American, 158: 72. (a one page article where the tracksite is reported for the first time in a scientific journal—other short reports appeared in Natural History and Life magazine at this time)

Prince, N. K. and Lockley, M. G., 1989, The sedimentology of the Purgatoire tracksite region, Morrison Formation of S.E. Colorado: p. 155-164, *in* Gillette, D. D. and Lockley, M. G. (eds.) Dinosaur Tracks and Traces: Cambridge University Press, 454 p. (more information on the tracksite)

Thulborn, T. A., 1990, Dinosaur tracks: London, Chapman and Hall, 410 p. (a comprehensive book on dinosaur tracks)

Archaeological and Historical References

Andrefsky, William, Jr. (ed.), 1990, An Introduction to the Archaeology of Pinon Canyon, Southeastern Colorado: U.S. Army Contract #CX1200-7-B054, with the National Park Service, vols. 1 and 2, 2192 p. (study supported by the U.S. Army and National Park Service to review the archaeology of the area)

Colorado-American Guide Series; Tour 9A: from the archives of the Colorado Historical Society, p. 302-303, p. 316-317. (a detailed account of Bent's Fort history, construction, description, and abandonment)

Friedman, Paul D., 1988, Valley of Lost Souls: a History of the Pinon Canyon Region of Southeastern Colorado: Colorado Historical Society Monograph 3, 122 p. (a history of the area from the Spanish onward with details of the native peoples' and settlers' influences and lifestyles)

Grinnell, George B., 1982, Life at Bent's Fort: Museum of Fur Trade Quarterly, 18/4: 6-12. (stories and folklore of the Bents' relations with native peoples and the construction and history of the fort)

McHendrie, Judge A. W., Origin of the Purgatoire River Name: Colorado Magazine, from the archives of the Colorado Historical Society, 5: 18-22. (narration on the origins of the name)

River of Lost Souls: The Denver Republican; Sept. 3, 1889. An interview of R.E. Talpey of Kansas City, Missouri. (frontiersman and native accounts of the disappearance of Spanish soldiers that led to the naming of the area)

Stoffle, Richard W., 1984, Ethnohistory and Native American Religious Concerns in the Fort Carson-Pinon Canyon Maneuver Area: Contract #CX 1200-3-A066, University of Wisconsin, Parkside, 268 p. (study funded by the U.S. Army through the National Park Service to review concerns and history of native peoples in the area)

Taylor, Morris F., 1964, Pioneers of the Picketwire: Trinidad State Junior College, 1925; Pueblo, Colorado; O'Brien Printing and Stationary Company, 69 p. (accounts from the first white settlers in the area on what they found in the 1860s)

Taylor, Morris F., 1959, A Sketch of Early Days on the Purgatory: Trinidad, Colorado; Risley Printing Company, 48 p. (a history of the area including another account of the lost Spanish soldiers and the various sources for the name)

Ward, Josiah M., Bent's Fort in Two Wars of the Union: The Denver Post; Feb. 8, 1920. (article on the Bent family and the fort's involvement in the history of the area)